stuff it

stuff it

THE STORY OF DICK MOTTA,
TOUGHEST LITTLE COACH
IN THE NBA

DICK MOTTA
with
JERRY JENKINS

CHILTON BOOK COMPANY
Radnor, Pennsylvania

Published in Radnor, Pa., by Chilton Book Company and simultaneously
in Don Mills, Ontario, Canada by Thomas Nelson & Sons, Ltd.

Designed by Donald E. Cooke
Manufactured in the United States of America

LIBRARY OF CONGRESS CATALOGING IN PUBLICATION DATA
  Motta, Dick.
    Stuff it.

    1. Motta, Dick.   2. Basketball.   3. Basketball coaching.
  I. Jenkins, Jerry B.   II. Title.
  GV884.M64A37   1975   796.32'3'0924 [B]   74-28178
  ISBN 0-8019-5967-5

INSERT PHOTO CREDITS
    Page 1   Photo courtesy of Mike McClure, the Chicago Bulls
    Page 2   All photos courtesy of Dick Motta
    Page 3   Photos courtesy of Dick Motta
    Page 4   Photo courtesy of George Carlson, the Chicago Bulls
    Page 5   Top photo courtesy of George Carlson, the Chicago Bulls
              Bottom photo courtesy of Mike McClure, the Chicago Bulls
    Page 6   Photo courtesy of Mike McClure, the Chicago Bulls
    Page 7   Photo courtesy of Mike McClure, the Chicago Bulls
    Page 8   Photos courtesy of Mike McClure, the Chicago Bulls
    Page 9   Photos courtesy of Mike McClure, the Chicago Bulls
    Page 10   Photo courtesy of Dick Motta
    Page 11   Top photo courtesy of the Chicago Bulls
              Bottom photo courtesy of Mike McClure, the Chicago Bulls
    Page 12   Photo courtesy of Dick Motta

To
the willing players, who've made my job easy;
the not so willing who've taught me;
my wife;
and Homer Williams, the one former employer
and friend
who really understands.

D. M.

and to
Gaston Freeman
in partial apology
for bad press
by a brash, young sportswriter.

J. J.

CONTENTS

I've never had a job in my life in
which failure wasn't predicted for
me.

What would I give for Walton?
My whole team . . .

Some of the players' agents are
nothing more than flesh peddlers.

I don't ask my players if they like
me. This is no popularity contest.

My team comes before my family, and my family knows that. And they understand.

I've coached in better leagues than the NBA.

There are a thousand law students who will be better lawyers than I am a coach.

You don't have to win everything to be successful. But you have to win everything to be satisfied.

—Dick Motta

PREFACE

WHO REALLY KNOWS Dick Motta? His wife? His team? His kids? Himself? None of the above? Dick Motta would choose the latter. He isn't sure how he'll react in a situation until the situation arises. But he knows he is competitive, and he thinks he knows why.

Motta is a miracle coach. Who ever heard of an NBA coach who wasn't over six feet tall and a former pro or at least college star? Well, then he was a good little high school player, right? No.

Then he made a name for himself as a coach at a big college, and moved onto stardom as the headman at a major university? Wrong again. When Dick Motta, coach of the Weber State Wildcats, was hired by the Chicago Bulls of the NBA, sportswriters enjoyed cracking, Dick *Who*? from Weber *Where*?

How did he become a pro coach? What bizarre series of events would make an assembly line worker the president of his company? Could a mechanic become president of the Ford Motor Company? Dick admits that he is the least likely candidate for a pro coach that anyone anywhere could think of. And he thinks there are 10,000 coaches who could do as good a job as he has done with the Bulls if they had the miraculous breaks he has had.

He's wrong there, of course. It's not often that anyone tells Dick Motta that he is wrong. But there are few coaches, even in the NBA, who could have done the job he has done in Chicago. Sure, his getting into the league was one zany chance in a million, but it took a man of unusual guts and savvy to take command of a dozen men, all a hundred times better athletes than he ever was. Motta is a psychological wonder. And a basketball wizard.

Is he the author of the previously quoted "Motta-isms" or were they taken out of context? The fabled Motta mouth has gotten him into more trouble than he ever deserved, and he is glad to have the chance to put all those quotes back into their proper perspectives and call off the critics.

Why is he defensive? Is he as independent and self-assured as the press would have us believe? Is he snotty and stuck up? I say no. I found him remarkably shy. A loner. Often soft. Frequently thoughtful. Terribly family oriented. Intimidating at will, winks belying scowls. A dichotomy. A fascinating success. Rags to riches, 1974. Dick Motta.

JERRY JENKINS
Wheaton, Illinois

stuff it

PROLOGUE

THE WALLS OF THE FIELDHOUSE at Wheaton College are bannered with the pennants of other small Midwest Christian colleges. The steamy gym in the western Chicago suburb is alive with rookies, draftees and free agents trying to catch on with the Chicago Bulls of the National Basketball Association. A couple of dozen pairs of Converse All-Stars grab the shiny floor chirp-chirp-chirping as the high-eye-browed hopefuls hustle up and down the court. They're warming up, hoping to be caught in the act of ripping down a rebound or sinking a pretty 20-footer when The Man walks in.

Dick Motta, readying for his sixth year as coach of the Bulls, is lounging in the locker room. Outside, under a 1973 August sun, collegians are puffing through the first week of football practice. Basketball seems a bit out of place. To everyone but the NBA rookies. And Motta.

Most of the rookies are black. All were high school and college superstars. Fantastic potential. The NBA has been their life-long dream. In college they swaggered, pumping up scoring averages and rebounding statistics with nary a grimace. Their teams followed them to tournament victories. But here they are nobodies.

They know Motta will not be impressed. He's seen hundreds of rookies come and go. In fact, he's seen lots of NBA *coaches* come and go. There have been nearly 40 coaching changes since he joined the league. Only one other coach has served with the same team since 1968. When he strolls into the gym in gray shorts (a bit too long, making his 5-9 frame look even smaller), the big bad superstars stop and wait for instructions. They remember basketball stories they read as kids. The guy who hustles, cooperates, gives it all he's got, he's the one the coaches want. They hope.

Motta calls the rooks around him at center court. A hundred or so spectators of all ages sit in the only section of bleachers pulled out from the wall. They will see little action tonight. Just drills. Motta will be separating the men from the boys. A few of the Bull veterans are also in the bleachers. The rooks know and steal a glance toward their future teammates. They hope.

The coach talks quietly, directly, in an intense monotone. His light gray shirt, with "Bulls" in red over the left breast, is already dark from sweat. His hair is combed just so, long enough not to be square, short enough for a Sears catalog model. He is a cross between Andy Williams and Robert Redford, a dead ringer for Senator Howard Baker of Watergate fame. Motta has even mistaken a newsclip of Baker for himself.

He holds a ball under his arm. "There are things here that you'll want not to do," he says quietly. The average height of the rookies is near 6-8. Motta seems younger than they, though they are just out of college and he is in his forties. He almost looks out of place, but his very presence demands respect. He never uses a whistle.

"Don't show off," he says. "We know who you are." He pauses and looks down. This is his bailiwick. He's in charge. "And don't read the newspapers. You may find yourself cut from the team by a sportswriter, but don't go packing your bags until you hear it from us. I don't tell reporters who will be cut. When we know you are not going to make it, we'll call you in and release you."

Motta lists a few rules, instructions for meals, rides, hours. Some of these ballplayers will be regimented more this first day of training camp than they have been since high school. Dick has a system, a technique. His success depends on it.

Phil Johnson, a stringy, 6-5 version of baseball's Joe Torre, will take the forwards and centers while Motta works with the guards. Johnson is a life-long friend of Motta. He has hollow, deep-set eyes and an intense stare. He's a youthful thirtyish, but his pleasant manner belies his demand for perfection. He's very much a Motta man and not ashamed of it.

Motta and Johnson are working at either ends of

the court. There are periodic stops in the drill so Dick can explain a play. A slim guard steals a glance at Johnson's end of the floor. "If you're not looking at me, I get nervous," Motta says, unsmiling. The guard is intimidated. "This is a tough game. If you can't take this, go home. Go home." When he likes the sou..d of the last few words in a sentence, he repeats them. "When I say *hold it*, you stop. Stop. Don't coast, don't dribble. Stop."

The rookies are fouling up the play. They can't get it. They don't understand. Motta is irritated. If they could see him wink at colleagues behind their backs the rookies would be more comfortable. But he wants them to know their places. This is all part of the try-out. Can you take it when the coach hassles you? The young guard doesn't move. A perfect pass eludes him. Motta swears.

"Where you came from, who you are, what you've done mean nothing," he shouts. "You're a rookie. You know nothing. You listen. If you can't take the razz, go home. Go home."

Mistake. Mistake. And another. "I could be home talking to my kids," Motta fumes, wrenching the ball from the rookie's hands. "I expect you to make mistakes, but don't make the same one too often."

By the end of the two-hour workout the rookies are exhausted. Then it's time for sprints. "Run backward until you hear the command. Then turn and run forward." A few times up and down the court leaves the ballplayers sucking for air, eyes bulging, cheeks hollow, faces pale. "You guys who finished first," Motta hisses, "you wouldn't finish in the top 10 if the veterans were here. If you don't think they're gonna be in shape when they get here Tuesday, you're wrong."

Motta was right. When the veterans arrived a few

days later, most were ready. More spectators filled the bleachers. In a defensive drill most of the players shuffle back and forth as directed. Veteran guard Jerry Sloan, Motta's choice as his most aggressive, determined player, gives the drill a little more. He raises his arms, staring straight ahead. He can sense the presence of an opponent with the ball. Jerry is 6-5, pigeon-toed and knock-kneed. He is working as hard as he will during the season.

Now the players are shooting around. Periodically Motta will say, "Hold it." On key the veterans stop, grabbing loose basketballs. The rookies quickly follow suit, dreading the Motta glare.

The coach is meticulous always. Half-smiling, sarcastic, expecting the best, he strolls around, bouncing on the balls of his feet. He stands at center court, surveying quartets of cagers laboring at five different baskets. He enjoys palming a basketball in his massive hands. His fingers are longer than those of many of his gigantic players. When he doesn't have a ball, his hands are together, fingers rubbing, twisting, working. His energy is released through his hands. ·

Motta keeps score, even in practice. He's daydreaming, imagining his team winning the NBA title. Oohs and aahs come from skinny black teenagers in platform shoes, high, floppy hats covering mounds of Afro naturals. They like the leaping fadeaway jumpers that pop the nets. Motta ignores the good shooting. Pretty shooters are a dime a dozen.

"Thousands of collegians can shoot with the pros," he explains, "but they'll be watching from the stands when the season starts because they can't run, move, rebound, bounce back. It takes that to play in this league."

None of the rookies had what it takes. Motta cut

them one by one, slowly. It hurt him to tell them that their dream would not be coming true, at least not in Chicago. He cut the last one just before the roster trimming deadline. He would stick with the men who had led him to three straight 50-win seasons, a mark he had always considered important in the NBA.

Three months later the Bulls are in the thick of the NBA race in the Midwest division. The Milwaukee Bucks, perennial winners of the division, irritate the Bulls during the first several weeks of the campaign, staying a game ahead. The Bulls win a record 12 straight early, but the Bucks also refuse to falter. The Detroit Pistons are a distant third, leading the hapless Kansas City-Omaha Kings. But Detroit is tough. Motta's game against them in Chicago, November 24, will be an important one. The Bucks would eventually pull away for yet another division title, and the Pistons would breathe down the necks of the Bulls till the last few days of the regular season, but Chicago needed this Saturday afternoon. It was important to beat the Pistons early.

The Bulls are scheduled to play on nationwide television at 1:40 P.M. Motta doesn't expect a good crowd. "With Michigan and Ohio State playing for a trip to the Rose Bowl today, who wants to see an early season basketball game?" He sits at the kitchen table in his Northbrook house. He's watching Kirt, his tiny seven-year-old, playing with the castle he got for his birthday the day before. Kirt's huge brown eyes bulge as he responds to every question with "What?" regardless of whether or not he heard the query.

"This is my girl," Motta says of Jodi, his eleven-

year-old. She's a fragile, lithe, soft-spoken little
charmer with feathery blond hair. Motta teases her.
She takes it well. Kip, the oldest, is at school, readying for a ballgame.

Dick reads *The Sporting News* article about his recent trade of Garfield Heard and Kevin Kunnert for
John Hummer. He smiles and shakes his head as he
reads that the reporter thinks it may have been one
of the worst trades in the history of the NBA. "Bob
Cousy (coach of the Kansas City-Omaha Kings) quit
last night," Motta says suddenly, staring at the
floor. He had no idea how that announcement would
affect the Bulls. Phil Johnson would replace Cousy,
with Motta's blessing, leaving the Bulls with a need
for a scout and assistant coach.

Before heading for the Chicago Stadium, the Motta
family will watch Kip, a freshman at nearby Glenbrook North High School, play a morning basketball
game. When they arrive, Glenbrook North is trailing
29-10 early in the second quarter. "Kip's team won
yesterday and we lost," Motta smiles. "Maybe we'll
win today."

Heads turn and people nod as the Mottas find seats
in the gym. Mrs. Motta, her blond hair cut in a neat
shag, is an attractive, personable woman who dresses
fashionably but not pretentiously. She has many
friends.

Kip is lanky and looks as if he might wind up taller
than his father. He has the same huge hands with the
unusually long little finger, a Motta trait.

During time-outs and breaks between quarters, little Kirt climbs to the floor and waits for a signal from
his dad. When Dick points a finger at him Kirt runs

around the entire basketball court, his birthday boots clomp, clomp, clomping. He gazes into the stands and all around as he runs, as if bored by the whole thing. He's very interested in how long it took him, and Dad tells him a faster time on each run so he won't get discouraged. Kirt seems tireless, ready to do it again after each run. He wears wrist bands around his calves so the new boots won't chafe.

Kip and the freshman Spartans lose, and with little time to spare the whole family is on its way to Chicago. Kip will be a little late starting his chores as one of the Bulls' ball boys. Motta says part of Kip's contract states that his father gets to coach the team.

The bright November sun of the suburbs is hidden by brown, tightly packed factories and apartment complexes as the Motta family weaves its way to Chicago on the expressway. Dick is used to the traffic by now, but it still bothers him. *Sure nothing like Utah. Everybody moving so fast, thinking only of themselves.*

Exiting toward the stadium, Motta drives under the El tracks, over freight tracks, into the dark area near West Madison Street. He jokes with the kids. Kirt tells knock-knock jokes and laughs before he gets to the punchline. The mood in the car contrasts with the dark streets. At high noon, on the slummy west side, Chicago is dreadful. You don't leave your car on these streets. You don't even wait long at stop signs. This area belongs to the people.

Motta's fingers are working on the steering wheel. He is beginning to think about the game, about the rugged Pistons, about big Bob Lanier, their left-handed center. The car is quiet. The streets are quiet. The mood becomes somber, dark. The NBA is bigger than Dick Motta and he feels it. It is full of big brown, ominous, echoing arenas, black hallways, night games, smoke-filled rooms. The Chicago Stadium, as are many NBA sites, is in the black community. This is the black man's sport. The black man's league. The black man's game. Basketball, say psychiatrists, fulfills the need of many blacks to reach up and out, to jump and run. And it's a game any poor kid can play with just a hoop and a ball.

Motta unabashedly insists that he does not see color on the team or on the floor. He has been accused of racism by blacks who have been traded from his club. Yet this day, and all season, barring an unusual trade or injuries, he'll start just one white player: Jerry Sloan, a guard. Center Clifford Ray, forwards Bob Love and Chet Walker, and Sloan's counterpart, playmaker Norm Van Lier, are black. Motta uses no quota system. He reacts to no pressure from "cause" groups. If his best five men were white and his seven remaining players were black, he'd start the whites.

He is just as hard on the black players as the whites. He's easy on no one. "I hate you all just the same," he says tongue-in-cheek. There's an element of truth to it. When someone loafs on him, Motta is quick to ridicule. He'll tolerate any mistake except loafing. "They're being paid too well for that."

The only safe place to park at the Stadium is next to the building, inside the fence. Management charges fans $3.50 to park. A decent seat will cost them around $7, so an evening for a married couple would come to around $30 including dinner and a sitter. "Now, more than ever," Motta says, "we owe that fan the best ballgame we can give him."

In the locker room the ballplayers are already bet-ting on a small crowd, what with the big football game and all. Norm Van Lier, the smallest man on the team at 6-1 and 175 pounds, is trying to give away a couple of his complimentary tickets to other players who might need extras. "When Van Lier doesn't use all *his* tickets, we probably won't have more than 300 people out there!" says Dennis Autrey, a curly-haired, 6-10 version of comedian Dick Shawn.

The Bulls aren't down after a loss the night before, though if they had won they would have tied the Bucks for the Midwest Division lead at 16-4. Now they are 15-5. With 62 games to go, it's too early to let losses get you down. The excitement of the new season is still there, but 10 games from now the grind will set in. Everyone will play with aches and bruises that would keep most men home from work. It's part of the game.

Things get quiet in the locker room about a half hour before the game. The players say nothing. Bob Biel, the trainer, deftly tapes ankles on a table in the center of the room. He wears dress shoes and sharp slacks but is bare chested. Expensive coats and slacks hang in the cubicles as naked giants slowly put on their uniforms. Van Lier looks tiny at 6-1 and 175 as Tom Boerwinkle (7-0, 260) and Bob Love (6-8, 215) stroll by.

The last of a dozen pairs of ankles have been taped, and Doc Biel begins cleaning up. Motta sits on the training table. The players don't look at him, but they are listening, motionless, save Clifford Ray massaging his surgery-scarred knee.

"I don't deny you the right to lose a ballgame," Motta says softly. "But let's not get in the habit of thinking we can always reach back and pull one out when we're behind." No more talk. The players sit, staring. Thinking. Motta leans against the table, hands in his pockets. "Let's have a moment of silence," he says, bowing his head. The players follow. After several seconds he claps. "Let's go!"

The players jog out to warm up. Motta shakes his head. "Lose a game like that last night—" he says, pressing his lips tight. Doc Biel is adding the finishing touches to a classy outfit, tie just so, hair neat. He's maintaining his reputation as the best-dressed trainer in the NBA. Motta, Biel, and security personnel joke with each other, but the coach is nervous. His hands are together, fingers entwined. He rocks back and forth. Between laughs he looks pensive. Suddenly he's up and gone. To the court. The game is about to begin.

Motta smiles nervously on the bench. Once the game begins there will be no more smiles. He constantly battles the refs. Not one call is ignored. If a Bull is called for charging, it's unfair. Every close call seems to go Detroit's way. Motta calls the refs by their first names, chirping away as they run past. Up and down. Up and down. There is no let up. The game is very physical, bump and run, push off and go.

"We're getting murdered away from the ball," Motta shouts to a ref. "C'mon, call a foul!" Sloan fouls Detroit's Dave Bing on a shot. "He never touched him!" In Motta's mind, every call really *is* against the Bulls. He wants so badly for things to go his way, for his team to get a break, for them not to make a mistake, that he sees the plays the way he wanted them to go. If Van Lier drives toward the bucket and someone gets in his way, Motta sees Stormin' Norman banging into a man who was moving, not a man who has established position to draw the foul. "He was moving," Motta will shriek at the ref. And he believes it.

He believes it every time he argues a call, but when he remembers after a game that he disputed every anti-Bull call, he knows that not all of them could have been wrong. But he can't be that objective in the game. He'd lose his competitive spirit. His edge. Every coach in the league fires barbs at the refs as they run past. The poor guys get it from both ends. Once in a great while Motta will speak in respect of the refs. But for the most part they *are* inconsistent. And they *are* incompetent. That irks the coach. His destiny is in their hands, and he can't do a thing about it. There are a few refs Motta respects in the NBA but some of the best have long since jumped to the ABA. Motta has been hit with technicals by almost every ref in the league. "I don't play favorites," he says, smiling.

"When the refs don't take their jobs as seriously as I take mine, that upsets me," he says. "And when they call fouls on my guys that they wouldn't call on Jerry West or Oscar Robertson, I don't understand it. Maybe I do. We have a reputation as a dirty team."

The Pistons lead 27-23 at the end of the first quarter, and the sparse stadium crowd is anxious for some action. The Bull starters hit the bench and Motta crouches in their midst. He says nothing. They say nothing. Yet they look expectantly at each other. Motta occasionally steals a glance at the Detroit bench where big, black Ray Scott is in animated discussion with his team. Pistons sneaking glances at the Chicago bench think the Bulls are plotting too. But they're not. They're resting. They know what they've done wrong. They know how to correct it. Nothing needs to be said.

Van Lier darts about the court like a phantom, sweat dripping from his full beard. He relentlessly pressures the Pistons, swiping at the ball, jumping, diving, backpedaling. During the next time-out big Tom Boerwinkle encourages starting center Cliff Ray. Cliff has had Tom's job since the big guy injured his knee two seasons ago. Tom would like to play more, but he is not jealous. He helps Ray, slapping him on the back, advising him, unusually friendly to the man who has won his job. Motta likes Boerwinkle. He thinks Tom is his best center, but he can't use ball-games to get his chronic knee back in shape. He'll stick with Ray who makes up for inconsistent shooting with speed and hustle and leaping ability.

"Next time down, get two on Butter's (Bob Love's) side without calling it," Motta instructs. (Love is called Butter because he loves buttered beans. He's the Bulls' leading scorer, a natural shooter.) Most plays are engineered by Van Lier who signals the play by holding up a number of fingers. The play works perfectly. Van Lier brings the ball across the midcourt line and works it into Love without signalling the play. Butter sneaks out from behind a Jerry Sloan pick and drops through a neat 15-footer.

The Pistons are still playing tough ball and the Bulls can't seem to get closer than within four points. With less than three minutes to play in the first half, the Bulls fall behind 48-40. They want to be closer by intermission, but Piston sharpshooter Bing is rifling in swishers from the outside. Motta thinks of the damage Charlie Scott had done the night before in the Bulls' loss. *Stop Bing.* The Bulls outscore Detroit 8-4 in the waning moments and trail 52-48 at the half.

The Bulls are halfway through the second game they've played in the last 18 hours. They sit at their cubicles, mouths open, breathing deeply. Their faces drip. No one moves. This is a time for rest. It's 2:15. Elsewhere Michigan and Ohio are fighting for the Rose Bowl trip. Someone could come in and report the score, but the Bulls don't care. They just want to rest. They guzzle Coke and Seven-Up from cans, replacing a little of the four to five pounds each lost in the first half.

There is no shouting, no chalkboard, no chatter as one might expect. Motta quietly reads the number of fouls each man has. "Do they call that slip they're running?" he asks.

"Sometimes," says Bob Weiss, the Bulls' third guard who has played in more consecutive games than any other active NBAer.

Chet Walker is old for an NBA forward. His black hair has specks of gray. It takes him longer and longer to loosen up after 12 years in the league. His legs don't stretch out properly until the second quarter, and pain stays with him longer. He sits staring, sweating. "Adams is taking off," he says without moving.

"Stay with him," Motta says. He turns his back to the straight-faced players. "We're down by only four. You have to stay close to these guys." He's silent for several minutes. The players are still breathing hard. "Get Lanier tired and he'll start fouling," Motta says.

Walker sighs. Ray coughs. Love shifts his weight. Sloan clears his throat. Van Lier purses his lips and scowls. The computers in their heads have told them that halftime is nearly over. It's time to play.

"Don't let down at the start of the third," Motta says, and suddenly they are gone.

Big Bob Lanier grabs Jerry Sloan after an unintentional trip and both benches empty onto the floor. Sloan is held back by teammates, but glares at Detroit coach Ray Scott. "I'll bust your ass," Scott snarls.

"You better come on then," Sloan counters. Both repeat their taunts. Motta rushes toward Scott.

"That's a little immature, isn't it?" he asks, hoping to shame Scott into breaking up the hassle, rather than prolonging it. Suddenly he realizes that he is eye-level to Scott's chest. He turns on his heel, a sheepish grin on his face, and sits down. Play resumes.

The Bulls, fired up, take command and grab a one-point lead. Lanier puts a couple of moves on Ray and scores. The fans want Autrey. "Cousy's gonna replace you, Motta!" shouts a fan. Motta never hears the fans. Never.

With 5:18 left in the period the Bulls are up 67-62. Van Lier bags his second straight long jumper to make it 69-62 and the crowd chants "Defense! D! D! D!" Detroit can't buy a shot.

Suddenly the roles are reversed. Detroit can't miss. Chicago can't hit. By the end of the third quarter the Bulls' lead has been shaved to one point at 76-75. In the fourth period the Pistons seem to have caught a second wind. They are playing a whirling-dervish defense, switching, double-teaming, and playing tight. With less than four minutes to play, the Pistons lead 96-88. Some fans are leaving. Motta calls a time-out.

"We've got to make up two points a minute," he tells the Bulls. With 3:30 left Love cuts the gap to six with a shot from the top of the key. Sloan forces a foul and a full minute later Walker hits to make it 96-92. Chet then rips down a defensive rebound and clears the ball to Love who connects on another two pointer. With two minutes to play the Bulls are suddenly back in the game, trailing just 96-94.

The Pistons lose the ball out of bounds and take possession with 1:35 left on the clock. Motta calls another time-out. "Don't force anything," he says. "Let's tie it quick so they won't have time to run out the clock before they score."

Davie Bing steals the inbound pass and scores on a breakaway. The Pistons are up 98-94 and time is fleeting. With 41 seconds on the clock, the Pistons regain possession. Another time-out. "Play the point of the ball tough," Motta tells his charges. "Try to intercept. We've gotta have the ball." There is no mention of the mistake that let Bing score on the breakaway. Motta is mad, but quick to forgive. His mind is reeling. *We've gotta get the ball.* Nothing in the world matters as much to him at that second as the Bulls getting the ball.

Six seconds later Jerry Sloan steals the ball and drives toward the bucket. He's fouled and quickly sinks a pair of free throws to pull the Bulls to within two at 98-96. Detroit has the ball. "We've got to play some tough D," Motta shouts. The Pistons stall the ball until a second remains on the 24-second shot clock. The pass goes to Lanier and he drops in their 100th point. With less than 10 seconds to play the Bulls trail by four. More fans leave the stadium.

Detroit plays a full court, man-to-man press. The Bulls hustle the ball downcourt as the seconds tick away. Walker, nicknamed the Ice Man for his cool under pressure, drives toward the basket and draws a two-shot foul. He drops in both free throws and Detroit takes the ball with eight seconds left, leading 100-98. They call a time-out to set up a play.

"Should we foul or try for the steal?" Motta asks, looking first at Sloan, then at Walker.

"Steal," Sloan says. "But foul if time runs out."

The Pistons loft the ball into play and Chet Walker barges in to intercept. The stadium crowd is on its feet as he dribbles toward the Chicago hoop. He is fouled on the shot and Motta calls a time-out. Walker will be at the free throw line with a chance to tie the game with two seconds to play. During the break, Motta makes no mention of Walker's impending foul shots. He talks as if the game is already tied. "Keep them from scoring and we'll get 'em in the overtime," he says.

Walker cooly ties the game with two free throws, and the clubs move into overtime. Bob Lanier and Walker trade buckets early in the extra period before the Pistons open a lead. Lanier scores three more points and Stu Lantz scores a three-point play when he is fouled on a breakaway layup. The Pistons lead 108-102 with 2:52 left to play.

In just over a minute the Bulls force three Detroit turnovers and baskets by Walker, Van Lier, and Autrey bring the Bulls roaring back to a 108-108 tie. Bob Lanier fouls out, opening the middle a bit for the Bulls, but the Pistons aren't about to roll over and play dead. Dave Bing puts Detroit back on top 110-

108 with a swisher before Sloan scores to tie it again for the Bulls.

Chicago comes down with a rebound and calls a time-out with 23 seconds left to play. They can run the clock to six seconds before using up the 24-second shot clock. When the scoreboard reads 0:07, Chet Walker scores on a driving layup, putting the Bulls up 112-110.

The Pistons race the ball to their end of the floor and pass to Don Adams. A questionable call charges Walker with a foul and Adams scores a pair of free throws to knot the score once again. With three seconds to play the Bulls have the ball in their forecourt and call a time-out. The score is 112-112.

"Let's set screens for Walker low and Butter high and get the ball to Chet if he's open," Motta says. Motta is in his glory. He'd rather win a close one like this where his coaching savvy is put to the test than win a laugher. He claims the close ones are hard on his nerves, yet these types of games are what his life is all about. He can't get enough of it.

The horn calls the teams back to the court. All eyes are on Chet Walker. Phil Johnson watches him try to get free to take the inbounds pass. Motta watches him. Even Kip watches him. The Bulls train their eyes on the Ice Man. Can he get the winning bucket? Detroit Coach Ray Scott watches Chet. The Pistons surround him. He's bottled up. The clock will start when a Bull catches the inbounds pass. Bob Love spins away from his defender and waves his arms at Dennis Autrey. The big center fires the pass to him, and as everyone else in the stadium watches Chet Walker trying to get free, Butter dribbles once and lets loose a high-arching 30-footer which ripples the net as the final horn sounds. The Bulls' bench erupts. Motta raises both fists and embraces Butterbean. The Bulls have won 114-112.

"You guys'll make an old man of me yet," Motta tells the jubilant Bulls in the locker room. "Hey, give me a break and win one by five once, huh?"

Ten minutes after the end of the game, the locker room is opened to the press. Motta often complains about bad press in Chicago, but it has to be seen to be believed. Dick enjoys the cheerleading he gets from Bob Logan of the *Tribune* who thinks the Bulls are the greatest team in history. And he's mildly amused by Bill Jauss of the *Daily News* who is constantly concerned that Dick might be misunderstanding the sportswriters. But Lacey Banks is the winner. The young, black sportswriter from the *Sun-Times* seems always to be cross-examining the coach. "Are you concerned that your free throw shooting is so poor?" he asks.

"No," Motta says. "There's not much we can do about it."

"You're not concerned with your free throw shooting?" Banks insists.

"Well, I'm more concerned that our opponents seem to have better luck shooting free throws against us than they do against the rest of the league. We'll have to cut down on fouls so they can't shoot so many."

"What do you plan to do about your opponents shooting so well from the line?" Banks asks, leaning forward and turning his ear toward the coach as the other scribes wait their turn to ask questions.

Motta's eyes twinkle. He winks at someone behind

Banks. "Well," he says, hiding a smirk, "we're gonna work on our free throw defense." Banks scowls, puzzled. Logan breaks in with a few questions. Moments later, Banks interrupts.

"I'd like to get back to this free throw defense," he says. Jauss, who has long since caught Motta's joke, laughs aloud. Banks ignores him. Logan leans forward, also seemingly interested in the free throw defense, but not sure what to think.

"Oh," Motta begins straight-faced, "We'll work on cracking our knuckles, rolling our eyes, and dipping our shoulders just when the guy shoots. And maybe we'll pipe in some simulated crowd noise." Jauss doubles over laughing. A smile escapes Motta. Logan grins. Banks scowls, thinking about it as he moves on to talk to the players. Motta was ready to take bets that he'd read about the free throw defense in the *Sun-Times* the next day.

"I have absolutely nothing against him personally," Motta confides, "But I'm convinced that anything he knows about basketball he learned on this job. He tries to stir up controversy between me and the players, asking us the same questions separately and printing our answers only if they differ. I hate to think he has the job simply because he's black, but I can think of no other reason."

After the game, Motta is high. He takes the family out for steak and lobster. At home, Jerry Colangelo of the Phoenix Suns calls and asks if Dick is ready to trade Cliff Ray for the Sun center, Neal Walk. "No," Motta tells him, "I'm not gonna break up the team when we're winning."

Motta would never do anything to a winning combination. The miracle coach is many things to many eyes, but he is above all a competitor. He will do anything to keep the advantage. Whether it's cards, paddle ball, or one-on-one, Dick Motta will challenge anyone. He may get beat occasionally. But he'll not lose. He'll not let up. He'll not give you a thing. On the following pages, he tells why.

CHAPTER 1

COMPETITION

ANYONE WHO BELIEVES that I really said I'd trade my whole team for the rights to Bill Walton is crazier than I would have been for saying it. How ridiculous would that be? Sure, Walton is great. And I'd give a lot for him. But who wants to bet on those knees?

So how did the story get around that I said I'd trade my team for Walton? I'm not sure, but I have an idea.

After a game in Chicago I was talking with the reporters as usual. One asked if I'd like to have Walton. "Hell, who wouldn't?" I asked.

"What would you give for him?"

"Why talk about it?" I said. "We're going to pick 14th or so this year, so why even dream about it?"

"But what would you give for his rights if they were available?"

"Oh, my team, my wife . . . I'd even throw in my father's lower forty." I laughed. The sportswriters laughed. Everyone in the room laughed. I'm no comedian, but I was happy with the line. For one thing, I certainly wouldn't trade my wife for anything. And what fool would give up more than a couple of starters for Bill Walton? But one of those writers was laughing only on the outside. I was quoted, as everyone knows by now, as saying that I would trade my whole team for the UCLA center. Jerry Sloan, Chet Walker, Bob Love, Norm Van Lier, Cliff Ray, Bob Weiss, Tom Boerwinkle, and the whole bench?

My father used to advise me to not make some of the ridiculous comments he'd been reading. Luckily, I was able to show him first hand that I am often misquoted. I was leading a coaches' clinic in Utah one summer, and Dad had driven up from Union to sit in on it. During a question-and-answer period I was asked what I would give for a championship team. I used the "My wife" answer again. Everyone laughed, including my dad. The next day he read in the paper of my marital problems and laughed again. The press enjoys misquoting me for some reason. I admit that my mouth has gotten me into trouble many times, and I know other coaches get bad raps from the press now and then too, but I guess my demeanor invites controversy.

I can't change the way I am. I don't want to. Oh, sometimes I'll see myself ranting and raving in a television replay and I'll wish I hadn't carried on so. But the next time I get in the same situation I find myself up battling for my team, getting nailed with a technical, and sometimes getting thumbed out of the game. When I'm coaching I'm a totally different person. I'm paid to coach a winning team, and I'll do anything within the rules to help the Bulls win. It costs me friends and reputation sometimes, but I can't help it. I have to be able to look at myself in the mirror and know that I've given it my best shot. I get a lot of kidding because of my size. I didn't mind appearing between Bill Russell and Wilt Chamberlain for the cover of *Sport*, but the article could have been more accurate. 5-9 and a half is small enough without having them say I'm 5-7. I think my size has helped make me a battler. Little people always have to work harder. What we lack in size and grace we have to make up in aggressiveness. Take Van Lier. At 6-1 and 175, if he wasn't explosive he'd never be in the NBA. And Sloan. He's a streak shooter, slower than most guards, less graceful than many. But he works, he hustles, he's aggressive. I'd take him over any "name" player.

I've been a competitor for as long as I can remember. I grew up in the 1930's on a truck farm in Union, Utah, outside Salt Lake City, and all I remember from day one is competing. My dad had 15 acres of vegetables which he and my mother and my younger brother and sister worked as a family.

Dad is an Italian immigrant, and mother was the daughter of a staunch Mormon. Her father was the 32nd child of a polygamist named Squires, who was Brigham Young's barber. My father wasn't the Mormon my mother was, but we went to church and were baptized.

My brother Steve is 18 months younger than I, so we did everything together. Playing cards was no game with us. It was war. I can never remember feeling good after losing at anything. The whole family was up at daybreak in the summer. Before breakfast my brother and I would stand my mother and father to see which team could tie the most radishes before breakfast. We would tie 120 dozen, count them, wash them, and box them while Mother and Dad started on the parsley. Then we would cut 100 dozen parsley while Dad started the irrigation for the rows we had just harvested. Mom would then start breakfast. Everything was a race. Everything.

We always wanted to see who could do the most. Who could finish a row of lettuce first. Who could carry the most cabbages in one crate. We did everything the hard way. There was very little machinery, so we had to work hard to turn a little profit. It was hard, agonizing work, and competition was about the only thing that made it bearable. People who enjoy little vegetable gardens in their backyards should try picking a whole acre of vegetables, bending over for hours in the sun. I don't regret the work though. My father supported a family with that farm, and the work made everything I've done since seem like loafing. Coaching in the NBA may be hard on the nerves, the hours can be exhausting. But hard work? No. I get paid for my hobby.

My father probably won't admit it, but I don't think he was ever totally happy on the farm. When he was 50 he went to work in a library. He loves to read. He would have been a great coach, because everything was a game to him. We all spent a lot of the time daydreaming. There was little else to do when you were bent over picking vegetables from sunup to sundown. I'm a dreamer now, and I'm sure it stems from those long hours in the field.

Every once in a while Dad would look up into the

mountains and get the feeling that it was time to go fishing and that we should take the five-mile hike, almost straight up, to Lake Blanche. We raced to see who could get up the fastest. It was harder work than picking, but for us it was fun. When I say everything was a game to my father, I mean everything. I can even remember his lining us up across the road to see if we could pee farther than the neighborhood kids.

We lived month to month for the Joe Louis fights on the radio. My brother and I fought every day. We listened to Notre Dame football games and New York Yankee baseball games. Johnny LuJack and Joe DiMaggio were like family members, we followed them so closely. Dad put a basketball hoop up on the barn and we played whenever we got a free minute, which wasn't often. One summer we dragged an old telephone pole into the yard and set up a backboard with an extension so we could drive and shoot layups without running into the barn or the pole. Dad has since paved the court and kids still come around there to play every day. At 68, Dad still plays too.

From the time I was six years old I loved to be outside, hunting, fishing, or just hiking. We had a loaded .22 on the back porch. Whoever was near it when pheasant or quail were in the asparagus would bag us something for supper.

I didn't like school much. Elementary and junior high were in the building where my dad had gone to school. During the summer of '72 I took my kids to see the old school. It's been torn down since, but I was glad to get to see it once more. I hadn't been there for 25 years. I showed the kids the little hallway where I first kissed Shirley Ferguson when I was in the ninth grade.

The teachers I liked best were the ones who let me talk about the hunting and fishing trips. When I close my eyes and think of the set of three lakes where we used to fish I remember only pleasant things. I'd like to be buried there. We'd take our poles, a loaf of bread, half a pound of lunchmeat, coffee, salt, sugar, and flashlights, and we were off. I try to get back there at least once every summer even now. My favorite rock is still there. Standing on it I can see the whole area.

What a fantastic break from farming those trips were. I felt like other kids were out playing and that we were slaves to the farm. It hurt to see my dad disc under a whole field of lettuce after months of work because we couldn't sell it. We would have to store and save all summer to make the one big paycheck last the winter. Dad treated us like hired hands on the farm, using whatever psychology he knew to keep us working. But when we went on our fishing trips, we were equals. He was happier when we were all fishing, and, of course, we were too.

When I was in the fifth grade, Dad let Steve and I miss two days of school to go fishing. I learned more on that trip than I would ever have learned daydreaming in class. Dad taught us survival techniques and living off the land. We had a great time, but I couldn't keep the secret when I got back to school. I told the teacher that I had been out sick, but she overheard me telling some friends about the two big fish I had caught. I'll take my son out of school for a week to let him go deer hunting with his grandfather. Some things are more important than a week of school. Anyway, in our family, the deer hunt is like a holiday. We never miss it.

Teachers who took us on field trips were always my

favorites. I always seemed to learn more when I was out in the woods. All I wanted to do was run and climb and hunt and fish. And compete.

There was one trip that disappointed me, and it still haunts me. My parents had talked about the fantastic Pacific Ocean until I could hardly wait to see it. Finally we made the big trip to California, and there it was. The Pacific. "Is that all the bigger it is?" I asked, incredulous. I don't know what I had expected, but certainly more than I saw. I wondered if anything would ever satisfy me. Few things ever have. I don't know what I'd do with an NBA championship. It's all I've dreamed of since I've been in the league, but I'm scared to death that I'll wonder again, "Is that all there is?" What will I strive for then?

My attitude hasn't changed much toward events in my life since that visit to the Pacific. I don't feel I have a very important job. I don't feel very successful. I realize how silly that sounds to the 10,000 coaches in this country who deserved the break I got even more than I did, but I really feel it. I'm awed by the fact that I coach a team that will play and has played against people like John Havlicek, Dave Bing, Bill Russell, and Wilt Chamberlain. But when I chat with them I find that they are no different from the kids who played ball for me in junior high and high school, and college. They're just like you or me. Oh, of course, they're giant physical specimens and they are basketball geniuses, but they're cut from the same mold. It helps me keep basketball in perspective. I've coached in high school and college leagues that had more balanced competition, better officiating, and less petty hassles.

I'll lose a game against the Lakers at the Forum in

Los Angeles and wonder when we're ever going to win a game there. I'll feel sorry for myself until I read about some kid getting his head blown off in southeast Asia. Then I realize how lucky I am. All I lost is a basketball game. Keeping it in perspective doesn't make me compete any less vigorously, but I could certainly have a worse fate than not being able to beat the Lakers in L.A.

Fans should keep the game in perspective too. It still puzzles me why a person would want to shake my hand and tell me, "Good game, coach." They treat me like some kind of a hero. I'm just a converted biology teacher working with some great basketball players, a grown man making money at a game. It keeps me young. I'm twenty-two years old today because I work and play and romp around and get a lot of money for my hobby.

I first bounced a basketball on a hard floor when I tried out for the seventh grade basketball team in 1943. I was small, but I was a pretty good ballhandler, and after having played on dirt, the consistent bounce from the gym floor was beautiful. I started all three years of junior high ball, but I was only the high scorer once. We won 12-9 and I had four. Shirley Ferguson, a cheerleader, gave me a hug around the neck after the game and I thought about it for three weeks. I was in hog heaven!

We didn't learn too much beyond basketball fundamentals back then. I don't think we had one set play. It was pretty much a freelance offense and we played alley-style basketball in the five-school junior high league. We were taught to hustle and to compete. I just loved it. My grades weren't too good, and often I'd be caught spearing fish with a pitchfork when I was supposed to be in class, but I liked school because of basketball.

Our coach may not have had all the basketball knowledge in the world, but he sure knew how to control his team. Once he cracked my head with another guy's because we were talking when he was.

The man who lived north of us on the irrigation ditch was the coach of the rival junior high basketball team. I spent a lot of time with him during the year, just talking basketball. I still see him often when I'm in Utah. Neither of us dreamed that I would ever be an NBA coach. I doubt if he even dreamed that I'd coach anywhere.

My brother and I had our last fight that year. We always played king of the hill on the bed, but we were finally too big to be smashing each other around the house every day. We were close and were best friends, and we still are. But that day things got a little out of hand. My Dad would yell at us and threaten to whip us if we didn't stop, but if we ever got beat, it was Mom who did it.

Steve was king of the hill that morning, so I charged him, leaping onto the bed. He bounced me off with a quick shove and I went reeling backward onto my head. I was furious. I jumped up and slugged him in the mouth, cutting his lip and chipping his tooth . . . and cutting my hand. He started crying. I tried to shut him up but he ran to Mom. She grounded me and I had to miss a day of practice before a game. Steve soon grew bigger than me, so I got smart and quit hassling him. We still wrestle a lot when we see each other. And we play a lot of pinochle. For blood. He's as competitive as I am.

I made the sophomore team the next year when I

started busing to Jordan High, a consolidated school that drew from the surrounding communities. It was a school with a little less than a thousand students, so I was glad to play freshman ball, as small as I was. I also made the soph baseball team, and sports were all I thought about. My junior year was probably the fastest year of my life. I was a happy-go-lucky kid and I enjoyed school and friends and athletics. I was outgoing and friendly and usually happy. I made the junior varsity basketball team and got to scrimmage against the seniors in practice every day. I could hardly wait for my senior year and my chance to play on the varsity. It became my 24-hour-a-day dream. I worked hard.

My grades even picked up during my junior year. Things seemed to be going my way. I figured that if I put my mind to something and wanted it badly enough, and worked hard enough for it, I could have it. I centered all of my energies around playing well in jayvee games and really hustling when we scrimmaged the varsity. I was still very small, and I had deficiencies in my game, but I was varsity material, and I knew it.

After the last game of the year the coach drove several of us home. I was last one on the route. When we pulled into the farm, the coach chatted a bit about the game. Then he shut off the engine and settled back in the seat. I really respected him and was thrilled that he would give of his own time to talk to me. ' Dick," he said, "you really want to play varsity ball n xt year, don't you?"

"I sure do."

"There are some things you're going to have to develop. Every chance you get I want you to work on your shot. Get somebody to defend against you and have him play you tough and tight. Get a high arch on that ball and get it over your man. Work on your moves. Learn to fake and stutter step so you can leave that man standing there when you drive toward the basket.

"Perfect your passing. Throw dozens of chest passes every day. You're not going to be a big scorer, but you can be valuable as a playmaker, a passer. Most of all, work on your defense. That's going to be the key to your game. If you can hold big scorers to a few points at the varsity level, you'll make it."

I went into the house walking on a cloud. His little speech was nothing out of the ordinary. Coaches now encourage kids that way every day. But it was a first for me. No one had ever taken that much of a personal interest in me. It was totally unselfish. He wasn't even the varsity coach. Why did he care so much that I made the varsity the next year? It really touched me, and I thought of it often that whole year as my brother and I played one on one for hours in the yard. We would have a new varsity coach the next year, and I was ready to do anything, sacrifice anything, work as hard as I had to, and compete with anyone to make that team.

CHAPTER 2

CUT

DURING THE LAST TWO MONTHS of the summer of 1948, I really stepped up my basketball program. The whole family looked forward to having me on the varsity basketball team. The words of the jayvee coach were still fresh in my mind, but what kept me going even more than that was the fact that he had taken the time to encourage me. He believed in me, and that made me believe in myself.

I didn't go out for football or any other fall sport because fall was such a busy time on the farm. I slept well every night, exhausted after a day at school, hours in the fields, and more hours playing basketball. I was happy. I looked forward to making the varsity. It was a great experience for me and helped me later when I could remember how important it was to me to make the team. I am always very careful in choosing my teams, taking into account the number of guys who would give anything to make it.

The football season ended and basketball tryouts were announced. I had improved on my skills and endurance and I figured I'd have a good shot at a varsity job.

Several guys were there, so the coach told us that there would be three cuts to trim the team to size. Everyone would be given a fair shot and a good look.

For the first week or so I was doing fine. Everything was working for me, and I was even shooting better. I moved well without the ball too and hoped I was impressing the coach. I survived the first two cuts, and I felt I was going to make it.

The coach was initiating a new program. The varsity hadn't done too well in the recent past, and as a new coach, he wanted to shake things up a bit and try to turn things around. I was catching on quickly to his new program, and there didn't seem to be a lot of good players available. I think he knew early that it was going to be a difficult year. Certainly there were no superstars to build a team around. I hoped we would gel and be able to hustle ourselves into prominence for the coach.

There were just a few days left before the final cut. I didn't want to take any chances. I couldn't let up. I played with abandon, even going for rebounds against the bigger kids. I'd been doing it for several days, showing the coach that I was willing to tussle with anyone to cement a spot on the team.

Then it happened. I raced through the lane and

leaped for an offensive rebound. I was bumped on the way down and twisted my left ankle. When I hit the ground I knew it was bad. Pain shot up my leg to my knee. Even my toes hurt.

I discovered later that I had chipped some bones besides ripping some tendons and muscles, but back then you didn't just run to the doctor and have something x-rayed every time you got hurt. My leg was black and blue from my instep to my calf. It was excruciating, but I had it wrapped and hobbled around, anxious for the mobility to return so I wouldn't have to sit on the bench too long.

I watched practice for the next couple of days. Then the coach posted the names of the players who were to remain on the team after the final cut.

My name wasn't there. I quickly read the list again. My chest was cold. A coach can make mistakes in judging talent, but he'll never make a mistake in posting the final list. I would realize later that three other seniors had been cut too, but right then I was thinking of no one but me. I stood staring at the list. I couldn't move. I couldn't even talk. Guys were crowding around the list asking who made it and who didn't. I looked straight ahead and went to wait an hour for the bus.

I tried to tell myself it was because of my ankle. I think I could have helped the team, but now I had no chance. I hated the coach. I hated school. I hated everything. I was so ashamed, so embarrassed. I don't know what it's like to lose a member of my family, but I can't imagine feeling any worse than I felt that day. After all the work I had put in, now I had been left out.

The bus dropped me off about four blocks from

home. I didn't really want to go home, but there was nowhere else to go. I didn't have to say anything. My parents knew I hadn't made it by the way I walked in. It was a sad day for them too. That night I walked out by the pole where the backboard hung. I stood there with my hands thrust deep into the pockets of my Levis. Winter was near and a cold wind whipped around my neck.

I had worked so hard, so long. I had done everything I could have done. Basketball was the one oasis from the classroom and the hard work on the farm. What was there to look forward to now?

"What's the use," I whispered to myself turning back toward the house. "To hell with it all." Everything I would do from that day to this would center around proving that that coach had made a mistake.

My whole life changed that day. I became a different person. I didn't trust anyone. Friends became unimportant. In a tree near the bus stop I had hidden a .22 which I used for hunting about once a week when I would cut school. My grades suffered. I became a bitter, untrusting seventeen-year-old. I lost interest in everything. I'm naive enough now to believe people, but I'm never surprised when someone tries to take advantage of me. Only a few people are close to me. I'm basically a very hard person and I don't trust very many people. I trace the attitude directly back to that day.

My whole senior year was a washout. I just went my own way and resigned myself to the fact that I would probably end up farming. Later that year I talked to the coach. He explained that my being cut was basically due to my ankle and to the new system which would have been hard for seniors to adapt to.

He just couldn't have waited for my injury to heal. It didn't help much, but several years later, when I was coaching at Weber State, he sent his son to play ball for me. It was the greatest compliment he could have paid me. After our talk I quit hating him, but my attitude toward life had been hardened, and it stayed that way.

Graduating from high school pleased my parents enough. I didn't even think of college. Steve was beginning to excel in sports, and strangely, I found that I was not the least bit jealous. I helped him and worked with him and he became a better athlete than I ever would have been. We had done everything together from working to learning to drive a car and working out. I was proud of him, and I like to think that summer I worked so hard to make the varsity helped him in some way to be the athlete he became.

My cousins had become farmers after high school and were developing a scientific vegetable farm that was to become one of the most productive and successful in the country. I figured that was good enough since college seemed like heaven to me. Farming still didn't seem too exciting, but I saw no alternatives. I had protected myself behind a wall of bitterness, and I just didn't care about anything.

Raymond Russell, who was active with me in the local chapter of Future Farmers of America, received a scholarship at the end of the year for $100 from Union Pacific. He planned to go with a friend to Utah State in Logan, a city about 85 miles north of Union. In late August, 1949, Raymond came to our house with the news that his friend had decided not to go to college. "We have our apartment all arranged and everything," he said. "Why don't you go with me?"

"Nah," I said. "I'm not going to college." It wouldn't have seemed more ludicrous if he had asked me to go with him to Russia.

"Hey," he said, "come on. Why not? We can split the cost of the apartment and do the cooking. It'll be fun." It started to sound intriguing at that. Raymond kept at me, harping on how great college would be. Finally I decided that I just might like to go.

"What do you think, Dad?" I asked.

"If you go, you have to finish," was all he said I was excited. Raymond had convinced me that I'c like Utah State. I would be 18 in just a few weeks an a freshman at a college with 6,000 students. I didn' know what to expect, but I was glad to be away froi the farm for the first time.

CHAPTER **3**

COACH

I WAS SCARED and homesick my first couple of days at Utah State. I had never been to Logan and didn't know my way around at all. A counselor signed me up for a major in agriculture and agronomy. That was nearly disastrous. I hated it.

There was no one to tell me when to get up, when to go to class, when to relax, when to study, when to work. I wasn't really mature enough to cope with all the freedom. About half the time I was in the gym shooting baskets when I should have been in class. I was having a great time and struck up a lot of acquaintances at the gym, but when it came time for the first quarter grades I was in trouble. A string of C's and a D gave me a grade point average under

2.0. "You have one quarter to get your grade point average up to 2.0," my counselor said. "You're on probation." I didn't even know what that meant, but it scared me to death. I still played a lot of basketball, but I also studied hard to get those grades up. All I could think of was my father's statement, "If you go, you have to finish."

I wanted to buckle down that second semester, so when our landlady offered me room and board and $40 a month if I helped her with breakfast and the dishes, I accepted. I was also involved in ROTC which paid a dollar a day, so I thought I was really rolling in money. Two weeks into the second semester, Raymond quit to go on a Latter Day Saints church mission and I was left alone.

Most of the athletes at Utah were there on scholarship, so I didn't really have a prayer of making the freshman basketball team. But I went out anyway, just for the fun of it. I was cut, but it didn't hurt since I was expecting it. Later, in the spring of 1950, I made the freshman baseball team and played first base and outfield. That made me feel good and I was beginning to enjoy college. Except my major.

One day in agronomy class the prof was reading from the text about making a hot bed. Hot beds generally consist of two feet of manure in a retaining wall with six inches of dirt on top. The decomposition of the organic material in the manure creates heat and prevents frost. But the procedure in the text would never work in Utah's weather. I knew that from experience. I raised my hand.

"It won't work that way here," I said.

"And just why not, Mr. Motta?" he asked.

"It just won't. It's too cold in Utah. I've seen my father do it, and he has to adapt it to the climate."

"Well, Mr. Motta, I'm sure the authors of our text have taken that into consideration."

"It doesn't sound like it to me," I said. I was right and I knew it. I won't back down to anyone when I know I'm right.

"If you don't like what's being taught, perhaps you'd like to leave," the prof said.

I laughed. "Well, I'm not leaving. Your hot bed may work in that dumb book, but there's no way the damn thing will work in Utah." He ignored me and went on reading. I was really discouraged and knew that I couldn't stay in my major for much longer. I spent more and more time in the gym again and was able to just barely get my grade point average over 2.0. At the end of the year I switched my major to physical education without telling my parents. I decided that it wasn't urgent that they know.

The switch to phys ed was the best move I could have made. I enjoyed physiology and biology and, most of all, getting to spend so much more class time in the gym. I got into a fraternity and I had found myself. I was still cold and bitter and distrustful, but inside I was enjoying college. I was leaning toward a career as a teacher or a trainer, and I studied a lot of physical therapy.

In one of my classes we had several weeks of basic wrestling. I had never wrestled before, but I seemed to catch onto it quickly. And I wasn't bad. The varsity wrestling coach opened his practices for challenge matches the first part of each week before the meets. Anyone who beat a regular at a specific weight class won his spot on the team. With only my phys ed experience behind me, I challenged the 147-pounder and won. I wrestled on the team for the rest of my college years and finished third in the conference as a senior. I thought winning a letter in something would help me get a job later.

The wrestling coach was also the trainer at the school and it was rumored that he was about to retire. I thought it would be ideal to put my wrestling experience with my desire to be a trainer and land his job, but it wasn't to be.

In my new area of study I was learning the rudiments and coaching techniques for all kinds of games from volleyball to the major sports. I daydreamed more than ever, seeing myself as the coach of a high school basketball team, or coaching all sports somewhere. I couldn't get enough basketball books, and I read constantly. I was very naive and didn't have any idea what it would take to be a high school basketball coach. I figured it was only a dream, since I hadn't played varsity ball. Maybe I could teach phys ed, but there was little chance that I'd ever coach high school basketball.

The head of the phys ed department called me into his office during my senior year and asked me if I would like to be head manager of the intramural program. I would be in charge of administration and would not be able to participate as a player. "This is the greatest stepping stone you can get in organizing meets, giving assignments, officiating, scorekeeping, conducting meetings, and drawing up tournaments. You'll have the whole shot. What do you say?"

I accepted. I worked closely with the faculty in organization and administration and I got some valuable experience. The department head was pleased, but in December of 1952 I got my orders from the Air Force to report in the spring for a tour of duty in Korea or Japan. Since I was headed for the Korean War, I made the mistake of not interviewing for any teaching or coaching positions after graduation. I was getting as many A's as C's by this time and my average was nearly a B.

After graduation and about four weeks before I was to leave for the service, my orders were cancelled. The U.S. had signed a truce. I had nowhere to go and nothing to do. Fraternity life appealed to me, so I thought I might stay and get my Master's and keep living in the fraternity. I liked the idea of being Joe College. I wasn't concerned about money. If I had a place to sleep and something to eat, I didn't care about much else. I didn't follow the fashions then and I don't now. I had a couple of pairs of Levis and my FFA jacket, so I wasn't too far out of it at an agricultural school. Staying there and maintaining the status quo would have been fine with me.

Monte Nyman, a friend of mine from the fraternity who had graduated the year before, had taken a job teaching and coaching at a junior high school in Grace, Idaho. He was leaving for a church mssion and asked to be released from the job. The school board told him that he was really putting them in a bind by forcing them to find a new coach that late in the year. The school year was about two weeks away. Monte recommended me.

I still didn't have a car, so I borrowed my father's and drove the 65 miles north of Logan to Grace where I met Homer Williams, the superintendent of schools. Mr. Williams, who was to become one of my closest friends, told me that I would be assistant football and basketball coach in the high school, and head coach of all sports in the junior high, as well as teaching the only seventh grade class. For that they would pay me $3,200, and if I wanted an extra $5 per day, I could drive the activity bus. We talked for awhile and Mr. Williams offered me the job.

Time was a problem for the people in Grace, so when I accepted, the superintendent had me type my own contract right there. I had a hard time remembering how to spell August, but somehow I banged it out. I had a job.

A 1950 Chevy was my first purchase, and I found a room in the home of a widow, Lilly Mather. From the first day of school until the end of the year I was simply run ragged. I taught seventh grade, the same kids all day. Being from Utah, I found it hard to teach Idaho history, and I wasn't really into math or English or spelling (can you imagine a teacher who can't spell *August*?). But I managed. I taught all three grades in a combined boys phys ed class, and then right after school I coached fifth, sixth, seventh, eighth grade, and the high school's jayvee football team in the fall. I coached basketball in the winter. Then I drove the activity bus and got home around 8:30 P.M. The days were full and I was always exhausted. I hardly had time to enjoy all my new coaching duties.

One of the seventh graders in that class was a lanky, dark-haired boy named Phil Johnson. He was to star for me in high school in a few years, then play for me at Weber Junior College, become my assistant there and with the Bulls before taking his own pro coaching job. Phil still remembers the day he walked into class and saw his new twenty-two-year-old *man* teacher.

Coach Motta has a way of talking that forces you to listen. There's a quiet intensity about his voice. He speaks in a monotone, but it's so direct that even in a group you'd swear he was talking just to you. He was always able to say exactly what he was thinking.

I didn't know how young he was, or that he was just out of college, but I was aware that he was energetic and that he was a man. Few kids get male teachers before high school. We considered ourselves lucky. The first thing I noticed was his interest in athletics. In phys ed he was always organizing teams.

He didn't favor his athletes in class, but we sure had a good time in sports. None of us could wait to get out of school and onto the practice field or into the gym. We sensed that he felt the same way.

Once he took all the boys in the seventh grade on a trip into the mountains. All the school would give him to take us up there was a short little bus with three seats in the back. We called it a chubby bus. It rained and rained the night we were supposed to go, but he just said, "Aw, what the hell? Let's go." We went sliding up those dirt roads, totally unaware of the danger. We spent the night in a cabin with Coach telling us stories most of the night. It was amazing. It was good for us to see him with his hair down, but he had the unusual ability to back off and not become pals with anyone. Back in class the next week, he was the same guy, in charge.

The main basketball team I was concerned with was the eighth graders. They were the junior high varsity. I moved Phil up from the seventh grade team to play, and the team really did well. I was happy with the record of my first real team ever. They were 9-1 and the only team they lost to beat them in triple overtime. Later in the season we beat them by 20 points on their own court. The kids who played for me on that team would be the high schoolers I was to return to coach two years later.

When we didn't have a ballgame of some sort on the weekends, I'd spend some Saturdays and Sundays at the frat house in Logan. I was single and lonesome, but often I took time to find the good hunting and fishing spots in Grace. One of the best trout streams in North America is right in that little town. I hunted deer and quail and pheasant. I was in school early to prepare my classes, and I was out late coaching, but when I finally got home at night I was lonely. Until Janice.

Janice was a senior in the high school. She used to come by when a little girl from across the street would wash my car. I got to know her during those occasional visits, and I found myself looking for mud puddles to drive through!

I had been taught in education courses not to date students, but I saw no reason for that. We were careful not to make any scenes. It wasn't like an old teacher dating a young student. We were barely four years apart. And we fell in love. After she graduated the next June, we were married (on the first day of the fishing season. That was the first and last time I missed fishing on the first day of the season!). I had my orders to report for Air Force duty in July, so it was good to have my wife with me. I told her that being the wife of a coach would be no picnic. She didn't know exactly what that meant. During the next few years she would sacrifice for my career, maybe more than she had bargained for, but she has never complained. She's been like a rock, willing to go wherever I go and do whatever necessary to keep things afloat. A good wife.

I went into the service as a second lieutenant, thanks to ROTC. Within six months I was a first lieutenant. I was stationed first in San Antonio, Texas, then we were in Denver for seven months before finishing up in Shreveport, La. I was in intelligence and found it very interesting. We didn't have any children during my tour of duty, so we traveled a lot in our free time. Traveling was good for us and the marriage, and we were glad to be able to do it. I played on all the squadron athletic teams and coached most of them as well. At Shreveport I coached football, basketball, softball, and volleyball and was able to get several months worth of experience working with players, many of whom were older than I. It would pay off later.

After 15 months in Shreveport, my active duty was over. Monte Nyman had returned to his coaching job in Grace, and he wanted me to return and coach at the high school level. Janice was happy to be heading home, and I looked forward to coaching my old junior highers.

Monte asked me if I would like to coach football or basketball. He had no preference. During the football season the kids would be off for a couple of weeks picking potatoes, and I wasn't too thrilled with the idea of coaching an outdoor sport in such cold weather anyway. That, I swear, is the only reason I chose the varsity basketball coaching job. Had I known how far it would lead me, and how much I would enjoy it, the decision would have been easier, and much quicker. When the football team was in the thick of its season and basketball was still a couple of months away, I frequently wondered if I shouldn't have chosen football so I could be more involved. Once I got into the basketball season though, I was happy with my choice.

Here was a real challenge. Take a bunch of high schoolers and make a respectable basketball team of them. Now I was a full-fledged coach, working the job I had dreamed about. Phil Johnson was a sophomore and probably wouldn't have played much had it not been for the trouble.

The team was playing about .500 ball during the first several weeks of the season. I was not happy with the record but the discipline seemed good, and I felt I had rapport with the players. I had strict rules, and morale was good. There were rumors that the athletes, specifically basketball players, were drinking. Homer Williams, the superintendent, told me that he wanted the drinking problem cleared up. I called the team together on the last day of December, 1955.

"I'll cut anyone who is caught drinking," I said. "Have your parties tonight, but be in early so you can make nine o'clock practice tomorrow."

In the morning everyone showed up except one kid. He strolled in about 45 minutes late and you could still smell the alcohol on him. I put him on defense for most of the practice and had him leading a fast break drill for the rest of the time. When practice was over, Monte played him one-on-one for about 10 points, then I did the same. After another hour and a half he was nearly exhausted. While I played him the last set of one-on-one, Monte went and cleared out his locker. I called the player into my office. He was sweating, huffing and puffing.

"Did you have a good time last night?" I asked. He knew that I knew.

"Yes," he said. "I did."

"We've cleaned out your locker," I said. "You're through." It didn't seem to faze him.

"When do I get back on the team?" he asked.

"What do you mean *back on the team?* I was very explicit when I said I wouldn't tolerate drinking, and I won't. You are through."

"Well, last year they voted on us."

"This isn't last year, and you knew the rules."

"Then how about—?" He named four other guys he said had been out drinking with him. My heart sank. I hoped he was lying. They included three starters and my scoring leader. I called in the other four. They all admitted to having been out drinking the night before. I was furious. I cut them all.

It was a miserable, uncomfortable time, but I knew I was right. Janice knew I was right too, and it was a good thing. She was about to go through some things that would make her less than proud that Grace was her hometown.

The superintendent backed me totally in my decision. Homer Williams and I became closer everyday. I trusted his judgment and I appreciated his concern. In a couple of years I would cut his son from my team simply because of lack of ability. We remained friends, and I still talk with him often, consulting him on many major decisions.

But the town didn't like the new basketball coach coming in and shaking things up. There wasn't much to enjoy in that little town of 700 people besides love and basketball. The school only had 180 kids in a four grade program, so there wasn't much left to choose from for a team. I enlisted a number of the sophomores and we finished with a record of 15-9. It was a humiliating year, but I couldn't complain about a bunch of sophomores who won 15 games.

The barber in town didn't want to have anything to do with me. I walked into his shop a few days after the cuts were announced and he said, "I don't need your business." I had to drive 13 miles to get a haircut. Janice and I had broken bottles strewn on our lawn, and once somebody threw two bloody, headless chickens in the front door. Half the student body cheered against us at home games. The team became more and more determined to do well against those odds. I wanted to have a winning, state-respected team so badly I could taste it. I began to coach with a fury. I wouldn't tolerate anything less than perfection.

I pushed the kids hard, insisting that they work and work until they had the plays down just so. It was a personal vendetta to avenge our treatment, and I was taking it out on the kids. As it turned out, having to use sophomores earlier than I might have otherwise was the best thing that could have happened to Grace High School. That year we lost in overtime in the game to decide a state tourney berth. The team that beat us finished second in the state, and the team that won our division in the conference finished first in the state.

The next season I had 10 juniors and two seniors who had already had varsity experience, and I felt we had a shot at the state title. No one else in town gave us a prayer. We kept our hopes to ourselves and went about the task of winning as many games as we could. Janice got involved and really made the team part of her life too. We had the kids over after each game so I'd know where they were. We would just have pop and crackers and stuff, but it became a big deal. Once one of the guys said he couldn't come because he had a date. He was one that I was most concerned about, so I told him to bring her. He did and that started a tradition. It became the biggest ego trip of the year to get asked to the players' post-game party. The parents got involved bringing food and the thing got so big that we had to move to a recreational hall.

We won so many games that the idea went around that the post-game party was a victory party. I had planned to have them after every game, win or lose, but then I started to like the victory-only idea. When we'd get down in the last quarter, I'd say, "C'mon you guys. If you don't win we won't be having a party." We didn't lose often.

We took a 24-1 record, a conference championship, and the new love of the town into the Idaho southern regional that season. We lost by three points to the eventual state champions. I sat down and cried.

Not having played high school or college ball was a point of embarrassment for me at that time and I felt I had things to prove with my coaching. I was just sick about the loss. I had prepared and read and studied and attended three coaching clinics. I talked basketball with anyone who'd listen. The town had turned around and supported us. Everyone had traveled the three hundred miles only to see us lose our shot at the state tournament.

Many times during the following summer Janice and I would look at each other across the dinner table and her eyes would fill with tears. I decided then that we would win the state championship the next season. Nothing would stop us. Nothing. That spring I was the assistant track coach and we won the state championship. I liked the taste of that title and wanted the basketball championship even more.

By the time school started the next fall, Janice was pregnant with Kip. I took her to the hospital at four o'clock in the morning, October 9, 1958. She was in labor until early that afternoon. I didn't figure there was much for me to do there, so I went across the street and watched a football game, getting back just in time to be there when Kip was born. (She appreciated that!)

That fall Grace played great ball again. We were 24-2 for the second straight year, won the conference and the regional and had lost just one home game in two years. Our only two losses came when our star, Phil Johnson, was benched with a sprained ankle. We beat the same team which had stopped us the year before and yes, we won the state championship. Phil was named the outstanding player in the state. He scored 32 points and had 30 rebounds. Little Kip, hardly as tall as the trophy, stood with us for the championship photo.

That remains the biggest thrill in my coaching career, bar none. Even after winning my pro debut before a full house against the Knicks at Madison Square Garden I told reporters that my biggest thrill was winning the Idaho state championship in 1959. They thought I was crazy. And maybe I am. There's nothing like a single elimination tournament with a gym full of screaming high schoolers.

I think coaching high school is tougher than coach-

ing college or pro, too. You can't recruit. You have to
take what's available and develop it. I enjoyed that.

By now I was making $4,000 a year and was
working summers for the school board. I poured
cement and helped remodel classrooms for a dollar
an hour. Pouring cement was hard work, but compared to truck farming, was like a vacation.

Phil graduated and accepted a scholarship offer to
Utah State. I asked for a $1,000 raise and applied for
a high school coaching job at Twin Falls, Idaho, and
the head job at Weber Junior College in Ogden,
Utah. I wanted to have something to fall back on in
case Grace didn't come through with my raise. I told
them that I would leave if I didn't get it. Homer Williams encouraged me to apply for the Weber job, but
I didn't think I was ready yet. I figured I'd have a shot
at the Twin Falls job since I had made a name for
myself by winning the state championship. Homer
insisted and pushed me to apply at Weber. (I think
he knew that the board would not approve my raise.)
He had 10 times more confidence in me than I did.

I finished among the top three applicants for both
jobs but was chosen for neither. Grace did not
approve my raise, so I had a rough summer. I decided
to finish my Master's, and looked for a good coach to
work with. Jim Williams, Homer's brother, at Colorado
State said he could work out a scholarship for me if
I came to help him. I had sold our home in Grace, for
which I had paid $6,000. I got $7,000 for it, so I
guess that was my $1,000 raise. I spent two quarters
as a graduate assistant at Colorado State before
transferring back to Utah State to finish up in the
spring of 1960. I was living on the GI bill during my
schooling, so things weren't too rough for us. The

fondest memory I have of those days is the confidence Homer Williams had in me. Even after winning the state championship I feared that maybe it was simply a case of having had great ball players. I thought maybe I had nothing at all to do with our success, I had no self confidence, but Homer believed in me.

Ironically, my brother Steve, after having starred in three sports at Jordan High, played football at Utah State, and then replaced me at Grace. Someday I'd like to work with him. He is the curriculum director for the armed forces schools in the Far East and he and his family travel all over the world.

Almost finished with my Master's requirements, I felt I was ready for another good high school coaching job. A new high school in Clearfield, Utah, a suburb of Ogden, was looking for a basketball coach, and I was intrigued. The school would open, as so many do these days, without a senior class. I would have another team of predominantly juniors and sophomores and have many of them for three years on the varsity. There would be school colors and a mascot and nickname to choose. It sounded interesting so I took my resume and my recommendations and applied.

The first question they asked was "Where did you play college ball?"

"Well, I didn't play college ball."

"Where did you play high school ball?"

"Oh, I graduated from Jordan High School in Sandy, Utah." Fortunately for me, they didn't press it. Now I'm proud of my record after having not played, but back then I was still very sensitive about it, even after having won a state championship.

I showed them my practice plans which were as

detailed and extensive as anything I ever used in
teaching biology or math. I told them as much about
myself as I could, starting with the negative. They
weren't shocked that I asked for total control of the
teams I coached, and they seemed to enjoy my candor.
"I am this way, and it is the way I have to be," I said.
"If you want me to coach for you, fine. If you don't,
tell me early so I can get the heck out of your way
and we won't waste each other's time." So many
people come into job interviews with their mask on.
I can't do that. They liked me and offered me $5,500
for the year. I accepted, and I was happy, but I was
not to coach at Clearfield High. It surprised me as
much as it surprised them.

CHAPTER 4

CATS

CLEARFIELD HIGH WAS STILL being built in April of 1960. Janice and I were looking for a home near Ogden, and I was completing the last stages of my degree. Then I got a call from Weber Junior College. The basketball coach they had hired the year before had quit while I was at Colorado State. They didn't want to repeat the whole interview scene, so they asked if I would come and talk to them about it again.

At first I really didn't want to. I was looking forward to coaching at a new school. Besides basketball, Clearfield wanted me to be an assistant coach in football and baseball. "Hey, last year you could have used me and I was desperate for a job," I told the Weber president. "I've got a good job now. I've had it only two weeks and I can't ask to be released from it now."

"We're offering $5,600 plus $1,000 for teaching summer school. You can use a car and a phone for recruiting in the state. If you want the job, I'll call the Clearfield superintendent and get you out of that contract. He's a friend of mine."

I told him I didn't think I wanted it, but that I would think about it. "This is really crazy," I told Janice. "Last year I really wanted it, and it has to be better than a high school job." She agreed. I called Weber and said I had reconsidered. "If you still want me, I wouldn't mind having the job." The president had already called Clearfield, and everything was set. One added bit of incentive was that the state legislature had already passed a bill which would make Weber a four-year school in three years. It would remain a two-year school for two years, then become a three-year school for a year, and then be a full-fledged college. I still had to finish at Utah State, and in September I would embark upon my college coaching career. Phil Johnson, who had finished his first year of basketball at Utah State, visited my apartment when he heard that I had taken the Weber job. "I want to transfer and play for you, coach," he said. The Utah State coach wasn't thrilled with that idea, but there was no changing Phil's mind. He would play for me one year and then transfer back to finish in Logan.

Since Weber was just a two-year school at that time, all the players from the national junior college championship team of two years before had graduated. I did have a few players back from the conference champions of 1959-60, so with Phil and a friend of his from Utah State, and a couple other good recruits, my first college team was a tough one.

There were no stars, but many of the starters were close to Phil in ability, so the team was really a cohesive unit. We were 11-1 in the conference and won the championship. We did well in the national JC tournament and finished eighth in the country. The season wasn't really as rosy as it sounds. In fact, after the first road trip, we were in trouble. I was having second thoughts about my coaching ability at the college level. Phil remembers those first harrowing days:

We won our first game at home and we were pretty high. We were pretty sure we would have an impressive team, so we looked forward to a six-game Kansas road trip. Our opponents in that six-game stretch outscored us by a total of 10 points. But we lost all six. It was good for us to learn how to come back night after night and battle to stay close, only to lose by a point or two. It could have ruined our season, but none of us were quitters. Especially not the coach. I don't think he's coached a team which has lost more than three straight since.

Phil returned to Utah State after that year, and the recruiting began again. To help out the athletic program, Janice and I opened our home to football and basketball players who needed scholarships. Since the school didn't give scholarships, I put the kids up at my own expense. We had two or three athletes living with us much of the time while I was at Weber. The night Jodi was born in late 1961, I was glad the guys were around.

The team had started fast and we were set to go on an 11-day road trip. Janice wasn't due for another three weeks, but the morning I was to leave she went into labor at about four o'clock. I was set to leave in an hour, so I woke up Curt Wilker, one of the football players, and took him to the hospital with Janice. At five o'clock I patted her on the backside and said, "I'll see ya." Jodi was born that day and I saw her 11 days later. Poor Curt Wilker was constantly mistaken for "Mr. Motta." Of course, I kept in touch with Janice by phone during the trip.

Finally I talked to the athletic director about getting the school to help defray some of the cost of putting up the athletes. "I can't do it anymore," I said. "I'm losing money."

"Yeah," he said, "someday I'd like to give you an IQ test. You'd rate right up there with the cross-country runners."

Weber Junior College won the conference championship and wound up 12th in the nation in '61-'62, but the next season was rugged. It was hard to recruit kids to a three-year school without a league schedule. We played any teams we could schedule and had a pretty good year. The best thing about it, of course, was that some of the kids with me the next year would be two- and three-year veterans. It paid off.

By the time we were a four-year school in the fall of 1963 and had changed our name to the Weber State Wildcats, we had enough experience to finish second in the big boy's league. Meanwhile Phil Johnson had starred for two years on the Utah State team which had made the NCAA playoffs both years. Phil was the team captain his senior year. He stayed one more year to get his Master's degree, and I hoped to get him as my assistant at Weber. Who else knew my system as well?

By now I was making $7,000 a year for coaching a very respectable college basketball team. No great shakes, but I had nothing to compare it to. People find it hard to believe that I really don't care that much about money. But I don't. I care about inequities, and I think all money situations should be fair, but how much money does a person need? I was happy and comfortable and my family had a nice home. I could sleep in a tent, seriously. I think most men could. But I wanted my wife and family comfortable, so we had a nice 20-year-old home.

Things were going pretty smoothly, but I really needed an assistant coach. Weber State agreed to let Phil assist me, but he would be a full-time teacher too. Neither of us could devote as much time to the basketball program as we would have liked. We didn't realize that we were on the threshold of a dynasty of sorts. I had recruited a big center, Gene Visscher, from Michigan, and spent a lot of time on the phone with him assuring him that we were interested and would take care of him. A good center is vital to my disciplined, patterned offense, and I didn't want Visscher getting stolen away from me by Michigan State or someone. I got him, and we wound up having the best team I would have at Weber, but we began with problems. Problems I should have foreseen. Visscher is older than Phil. Not by much, but by enough.

Visscher had played a lot of high school, junior college, and service ball, and maybe in recruiting him we had made him feel like our great white hope. He was to become our leading scorer and rebounder and make the all-conference team for two years, and the 'Cats would win consecutive league titles with him at center. During an early, pre-season workout, Phil was working with Gene on an inside pivot.

A few minutes later Visscher was frustrated. "This move isn't going to work anyway," he said.

Phil slammed the ball to the floor. "You know so much, do it yourself," he snapped. I ignored the encounter until after practice when I called Visscher into my office. I was furious, but Gene wasn't the type who needed a harsh chewing out. I had the feeling he already knew he'd been wrong.

"When Phil tells you something, I expect you to respect him as you would me," I said. "When he talks to you, you can assume it's me talking. You know I wouldn't tolerate any backtalk." Visscher apologized to Phil, and Phil conceded that he shouldn't have blown up at him. They never had another conflict. In fact, after I left Weber a few years later, Phil became the head coach and hired Gene as his assistant. And when Phil joined me in Chicago a couple of years after that, he recommended Gene as his replacement at Weber.

With a young and knowledgeable assistant who really knew my program, and a scoring center surrounded by a balanced bunch of defensive-minded starters, we had a great 1964-65 season. We were 22-3 and won the conference championship. After five years at Weber I hadn't had a losing team, or even one which finished lower than second in the league. Often I wondered if I had what it took to coach a major university team. I was still sensitive about not having played high school or college ball, and I wondered what kind of a break I might need to get into a bigger school. But I didn't worry about it. I was content at Weber and, when I considered the possibility that I might coach there until I retired, the thought didn't sound too bad at all. At least not until I found out what Weber State was paying to get a new football coach.

The football program had been losing thousands of dollars every year, and basketball and a few other money-making sports were carrying the athletic program financially. With Brigham Young University, Utah, and Utah State also vying for the best high school prospects in the state, I figured we had done well recruiting. People outside the state were beginning to know how to pronounce Weber (it's Weé-bur, not Webb́-er). I wanted to think that our successful basketball teams had a lot to do with that. When the officials called me in and told me I was going to get a raise to $11,000 so I would be at the same level of the new football coach, I balked.

"Hell, I've been here five years and we've won 20 games a year," I said. "I've got a good program going here, and I'm supposed to make the same as a football coach who hasn't proved himself? I can't accept that."

I didn't get any more money than they offered, but they did make some important concessions. They said I could be a full time coach, without worrying about teaching five classes. The catch was that I would have to give up my academic rating and my tenure. In other words, I'd be getting hazard pay. If I had a losing season or two, I couldn't depend on my seniority to keep my job at the school. That didn't bother me. Most coaches have little security. I looked forward to being able to give my whole day to the team. We were successful before, so we should easily do as well now.

I still hadn't come to the point where I took my

coaching ability for granted. I'm still not at that point. I know I've got an image in the press of a brash, stuck-up, know-it-all, but I'm not. I'm going to get fired some day, and I don't like that. I work hard and push myself and my team so that won't happen. Some people think I could sit back and say, "Hey, I know some basketball." It would be more logical to say that I believe in my teaching methods. Repetition is the secret to my teaching. But coaching? The driving force behind my coaching is that I'm afraid I'm not going to win a game and people will realize that I'm just a biology teacher who miraculously wound up in the NBA. Most of the stuff I use is taken from other coaches. I don't watch them coach, ever. But I read their books. And I go to their clinics.

During Gene Visscher's senior year, '65-'66, we were co-champs of the conference and finished 21-5. I got a thousand dollar raise and decided to treat myself to my third car, the first brand new one I had ever bought. In spite of my coaching insecurity, Janice and I began thinking about a new house. And maybe a new boy. Yes, we knew exactly what we wanted. We had talked frequently about adoption, but now we were serious. Kip and Jodi were old enough to be doing many things for themselves, and we became anxious to have a baby in the house.

We had known of a couple of underprivileged kids in Grace, Idaho, and had looked into the possibility of adopting them. The authorities were looking only for foster parents, so nothing ever came of it. We didn't want to love a couple of kids for a few years and then have to give them up. We wanted another son of our own.

I wasn't sure what motivated me to want to adopt.

But the agency wanted to know. I liked the social worker. She was direct and blunt. After first applying to adopt, we had three more interviews with her a month apart each. That's a cooling-off period so they could see if we lost our enthusiasm or if the novelty of the idea wore off. In a way, she tried to see if she could talk us out of adopting. If we wavered, she'd have disqualified us. We didn't waver.

"Why are you adopting?" she asked.

"I don't know," I said. "Really I always wanted to have a large family. Now I'd at least like to have two boys."

"Is there any pity involved in your decision to adopt?" she pressed. "Do you have the idea that by adopting you're going to do some poor child a great service?"

"Not exactly, but I suppose that does enter into it a bit."

"Well, forget that," she said. "It doesn't work that way. The child you adopt will be giving you more than you give him. You should force yourself to realize that. It will help you love him rather than pity him."

We agreed. She asked if we cared if the child was deformed or handicapped. We didn't. "I just want a boy," I said. They checked us out pretty thoroughly, visiting the house, checking former acquaintances, the whole bit. We figured it would be at least a six-month wait after our last interview. It was more exciting than having one of our own. When Kip and Jodi were born we were thrilled, but the excitement was controlled because we knew it would take close to nine months. We could see the development as Janice came closer to the time of delivery, so we had it pretty well scheduled. But with our new boy, we didn't know what to expect from day to day. They said they'd call us. We didn't like to be away from the phone much. Have they called yet? was the unasked question everyday.

I was excited about the 1966-67 season because I had been able to recruit one of my top prospects. Dan Sparks had visited the campus and I had assigned Gene Visscher to entertain him. Gene was as happy as anyone about playing at Weber, so I just hoped he could transfer some of that enthusiasm to Sparks. I guess Gene didn't understand how important it was to us to get Sparks. The night he took him out I told him to call me as soon as he got in to tell me how he thought things went. At about 10 o'clock that night I got antsy. I called Visscher's place.

His wife answered. "They're not back yet," she said. "Yes, I'll have him call as soon as he gets in."

I don't remember how many times I called that night, but Gene does. When he got home, well after midnight, his wife told him that I had called about every 20 minutes or so for several hours. "He said you should call him as soon as you get home, no matter what time it is."

"Oh, I can't call him now," Gene said. "It's late. He'll be in bed."

"Gene, every single time he called he reminded me to have you call as soon as you got in." Visscher figured I'd be mad if I waited up a long time and he didn't call. But he figured I'd be more upset if he woke me up, just to tell me everything seemed fine with Sparks. He didn't call. I waited up until 4 o'clock, and I hassled Visscher a bit when I got up.

"Quit worrying, coach," he said. "I got him. He's coming."

"I hope you're right," I said. "Are you sure?"

"Well, I've got to go by his word. You've got to get his name on the line."

Sparks stuck by his word. After his second year at Vincennes Junior College he replaced the graduating Visscher and played two years at Weber State. He would play a couple seasons in the ABA before returning to Vincennes to be the assistant coach.

We didn't win the conference the first season Sparks was with us, but I can't forget that year because it was when we got Kirt. Just 20 days after our last interview, the social worker called. "The baby is ready," she said.

We had just played a doubleheader against Idaho State, and I had a practice scheduled. "Listen," I said, "Can my wife take care of that?" I knew when I said it that it was a mistake.

"No, you both have to be here," she snapped.

"Well, I'm in the middle of a job here," I said.

"Well, if your job is more important to you than this boy, you'd better just forget it." For the first time, I turned a practice over to Phil, and Janice and I flew to get the new member of our family. It was a strange feeling to know that you could accept or reject a human being. There was no way we would have rejected him on the basis of looks. Tiny babies all look the same to me.

We left Kip and Jodi at my parents. My father wasn't too thrilled with the idea of adopting. "It just isn't right to have someone else's child," he said. We didn't worry at all about that. The agency kept from us all the details about the birthplace, parents, and anything else we didn't need to know. And that's the way we wanted it. From the minute we saw the baby, it was ours alone. We had assured Kip and Jodi, then 8 and 4, that they were not adopted. I call Kip my firstborn and Jodi my only daughter, "the best girl in the world." Kirt is our miracle boy.

When we got back to my parents' place, I handed Kirt to my dad. He held him for two or three minutes. Then he said, "This is the greatest thing that could have happened. I'm glad I talked you into it."

We have never hid from Kirt the fact that he's adopted. The last thing we wanted was for him to find out from someone other than us. We've told him all along that he's special because we chose him.

I've always played rough with him. One night when he was about three years old I was putting him to bed. After he said his prayers I took him by the shoulders and bounced him up and down. He was giggling. He seldom cried and always seemed so happy. He talked early and seemed so intelligent that we thought he might be gifted. I don't know exactly how that is measured, but we know he's very quick and perceptive for a young boy. When I stopped bouncing him his brown hair was flopped over his forehead, and he grinned.

"You know," I said, suddenly serious, "it's a miracle that we got you. You're my miracle."

A few days later he came down to the breakfast table and asked me, "Am I still your miracle?"

"Yup, Kirt," I said. "You're my miracle."

He looks so much like the rest of our family that people comment about it all the time. "He sure looks like his dad, doesn't he?" they ask. He *does* look like me.

I had no idea that the 1967-68 season would be my last at Weber State. I had gotten another thousand dollar raise and we had moved into a beautiful, custom-built home. I knew Dan Sparks would be coming into his own as a senior, and this was the year that a conference championship could actually get us into the NCAA playoffs. I was excited and ready.

Our first game was against Pan American, so I knew there would be pro scouts there. Pan American had a promising center named Otto Moore (who wound up in the NBA) and the scouts wanted to see how he would do against a good defender like Sparks. We blew Pan American off the floor. In our booster club room after the game a man introduced himself to me as Dick Klein, owner, general manager, and president of the Chicago Bulls. I was impressed.

I had never met anyone from the NBA, and I hadn't even seen a pro game except on television. Klein had been there to see Otto Moore and had been intrigued by our play. He asked if Phil and I and a couple of others would join him for dinner. We spent about three hours at a steak place, and talked about the NBA. At about midnight, I reminded Phil to make a bedcheck. "You run that tight of a ship here?" Klein asked.

"What kind of rules do the pros have?" I asked. "Is there any discipline? Does playing for money change a player? Are they coachable? How can they possibly play 82 games in a season?"

It was an enjoyable evening. I got a taste of the NBA from this cashmere-coated executive.

Late in the season we were really rolling. We swept to the conference championship and suddenly we had earned a spot in the NCAA playoffs. In a frame on my wall is our team slogan from that season: "We worked for it, we deserved it, it's ours." We made the qualifying rounds and played New Mexico State for the right to play UCLA. And this was during the Lew Alcindor (Kareem Abdul-Jabbar) era. The preliminary game to ours was Houston against Loyola of Chicago. I was tempted to ask those coaches for their autographs!

We led New Mexico State by three with about six minutes to play. Phil and I looked at each other. "Hey," I said, "we didn't want to win this game, we just wanted to look respectable!" So, we started coaching instead of watching, and we lost. Actually, what happened was something we would probably do again, though I don't often admit that in front of Phil. He had scouted New Mexico State and felt that our zone trap would be effective against them. It probably should have been, but New Mexico was exceptionally hot. They hit three or four long jump shots to beat us. In a way it proves that scouting doesn't make that much difference, but that's not fair to Phil. I've always said that a team that can beat you from the outside deserves to win.

The year had been historic with the NCAA berth and all. It meant nothing but good things ahead for Weber. I would be getting a two thousand dollar raise to $15,000 for the next year, our adopted son had won our hearts, and we were content in our new home.

I had been recruiting a young player from El Paso named Nate Stephens. I'd been in contact with him since he'd been a sophomore in high school. Just after the end of our season in early 1968, Nate had second thoughts. Texas Western had sought the aid of the Dallas Chapparells of the ABA in getting Nate to play for their school. Dallas had written him a letter, encouraging him to go to Texas Western where he would be groomed for the pros and from which they would draft him into the ABA.

It sounded good to Nate, so he leveled with me. I had to admit that it was pretty good recruiting, and totally legal. I began to wonder if maybe Dick Klein could help me out. "This is Dick Motta from Weber State," I said when I reached him. I explained the situation. Klein said he would not only write Stephens, he would call him and recommend Weber because of our training and discipline. I guess he'd been impressed with our bedchecks. The strategy worked. Stephens decided to come to Weber.

A few months later I was sitting at home, figuring the possibilities of the upcoming season. It was mid-May and three-fourths of my recruiting was done. The whole family was home and quiet as I penciled lineup combinations on several sheets of paper. At eight o'clock the phone rang.

"This is Dick Klein, Chicago Bulls. Did you get Nate Stephens?"

Stephens had signed a letter of intent. I said, "Yeah, he's on contract."

"How would you like a different contract?" Klein said.

"No, that's all he can get. Board, room, tuition, fees, and $15 a month. We've given him our best deal."

"I don't mean him," Klein said. "I mean you."

"What?"

"How would you like to come to Chicago and be the head coach of the Bulls?"

It sounded like Klein, but now I wasn't sure. I'm not above pulling practical jokes, and I thought someone might be getting back at me for one. "Who is this?" I asked.

"You know who it is. If you're interested in the job, call me back in an hour."

CHAPTER 5

CONTEMPLATION

AS I HUNG UP THE PHONE, the first thing that hit my brain was that I had a nucleus of at least two super ballplayers for the upcoming college season. Willie Sojourner would be a sophomore, and Nate Stephens would join us. There were some other good kids returning from our NCAA playoff team, and I felt we were just one player away from breaking into prominence in the university division.

I needed more scholarships. And it would help if Phil could be relieved from some of his teaching duties so he could be my full-time assistant. Maybe this offer from Chicago would shake things up at Weber and I would have something to bargain with. Deep in the back of my mind I wondered if I could really coach in the NBA. It was ludicrous.

"This can't be real," I said to Janice. She and I talked for about an hour. Coaching professional basketball was beyond my wildest imagination, and *I'm* a daydreamer. I imagined myself coaching an NCAA winner. And I imagined myself getting a job at a major university. But I never even thought about the NBA. "It's ridiculous, and it'll never happen," I said. "But maybe I can use it as a wedge here."

One minute I wanted to be flattered by the offer, and the next I chastised myself mentally, knowing that Klein must have been terribly desperate to offer me the job. But then, it might be fun to see how I could do with a team of professionals. Nah, it'll never happen. I wrote down a few questions and called Klein out of curiosity. I wasn't sure I'd ever talk to him again, so I called collect.

"I wasn't really just scouting Otto Moore last December," Klein told me. "I was looking for a coach too. I saw a lot of ballgames last season, and several of them were yours. I knew by Christmastime that I was going to offer you the job." The Bulls had been in existence just two years, and Chicago scout Jerry Colangelo was taking coach Johnny Kerr with him to Phoenix where they would be general manager and coach.

"Let me get this straight," I read from my list, "If I were to take this job, you'd seriously give it to me?"

"Yes."

"It would be mine?"

"Yes. I have total authority. I have already cleared it with my board of directors. I have talked to one other coach, but you are my main choice. You are the guy we want."

"That's ridiculous. You don't even know me."

"I've been following you. I've sneaked into four or

five of your games. We'll give you $45,000 for two years." That would be $7,500 more per year than I would make at Weber. I didn't need it or want it.

"I don't think so," I said. "What makes you think professional ballplayers would let me try to coach them."

Klein talked for a couple of hours discussing the pros and cons of the Bulls. He talked about the players he had, and the ones he thought he could get through trades and drafts. He honestly believed that he was a half a player away from a world's champion- ship. I asked him mundane questions, to me hypo- thetical questions. Would you move me? Could my family stay here so the kids could stay in school? When would I have to be there? He answered all the questions with answers I wanted to hear, as a crafty salesman would do. I was looking for an out. I was not believing that he could be fool enough to offer me the job. It made about as much sense as offering the bank presidency to a teller with two weeks' ex- perience. I knew I wasn't fool enough to accept it.

"There is just no way I can give you any kind of an answer," I said.

"I don't expect you to," he said. "We would like you and your wife to visit Chicago. Arrange a flight and bill it to the Bulls. Then call me and tell me when you'll arrive."

Ever so gradually I let the possibility dance on my brain that I might have the ability, that I might be worthy of being offered such a job. But the thought didn't last long. I would accept the trip to Chicago so Janice and I could get away for a few days. And, by going, perhaps I could prove to Weber State that someone else was interested in me and I could get a few more scholarships. Those were the only two reasons I called Klein back and told him we would fly into Chicago the next Thursday.

"Now not a word of this to anyone," he said. "Who'd believe I'm hiring Dick Motta from Weber State anyway?" I knew that all too well. I could have shouted it from the rooftops and no one would have printed it.

Imagine yourself calling your father or mother and telling them that you're going to interview for a better job. But it's not just a promotion. It's the top job available in your field, two, three, or five jumps ahead of where you should be at this stage of your career. Imagine the reaction. Had I told my father I was going to interview at Utah State, or the University of Michigan, he'd have been thrilled. But the Chicago Bulls? There was a moment of silence. "There's something wrong with that," he said. "It's not just logical." He was right. I assured him that I was not seriously considering it. I had never had a losing season. My record at Weber was 164-50 and we had won a bunch of titles. But that was nothing compared to some of the coaches I knew.

Janice and I landed at O'Hare Field, the world's busiest airport, at the world's busiest time. I think every car and plane in the country passes through Chicago on its way home during the evening rush. I was nervous as we stepped off the plane. It seemed that half the population of Utah was scurrying up and down the corridors at O'Hare. The airport was bigger than the town I'd been born in. I had never felt so out of place. Everyone was in a hurry. The Bulls' business manager, Riley Morgan, met us as we headed for the baggage claim. I could tell the minute he laid eyes on us that he felt Klein had blown his cork. Klein had probably built me up to him to justify his seeming stupidity at hiring a nobody. Whatever, I didn't live up to Morgan's mental image. He stood staring at me in all my 5-9, crewcut splendor. He had psyched himself up to be enthusiastic and to help Klein sell me on the job, but by the time we reached the baggage claim area, he had run out of conversation. *Yes, the weather is fine out in Utah. No, it's not quite so humid as it is here. Yes, the flight was fine. Yes, we ate on the plane. No, we're not too tired. Yes, we're looking forward to seeing Mr. Klein again.*

I was sorry to have disappointed Riley. I'm not sure what he had expected. What are coaches supposed to look like?

There aren't many freeways in Utah. It seemed we were crawling eight abreast out of O'Hare and up the north shore to Evanston. Being in the backseat I couldn't keep my eye on the road as much as I would have liked either. Chicago is the only place in the world where you can drive 20 minutes without leaving the scene of an accident.

When we got to the hotel, Riley took over at the front desk. "Reservation for the Johnsons," he said. Janice and I looked at each other. It would have been more secretive to register us as the Mottas. Not a soul in Illinois, outside the Bulls, had ever heard of us. But this was Klein's cloak and dagger game.

Morgan was no longer trying to sell me at all. He came up to the room and we talked about player personnel for awhile, but he was just following orders. Just going through the motions. We were getting hungry.

"Go to bed," Riley said. "Sleep well. Klein will meet you here at 10 o'clock in the morning."

We didn't feel like sleeping. I was pent up, and Janice was just a bit confused and amused. Somehow I guess we had expected a more formal greeting. Or a midnight meeting or something. But to be hustled off to bed? Maybe they had lost interest in me already. I had no intention of taking the job, but it would have hurt to have them turn me down before I turned them down. Janice and I decided to go for a walk.

We weren't far from the Northwestern University, so we strolled through the campus. It was nice. And peaceful. But I wasn't. I was a little excited, but mostly feeling bad that I was wasting Klein's time and money just for a wedge at Weber. But then, he *had* invited me.

We stopped at a sidewalk cafe outside the hotel to get a sandwich. As we waited for our order, I noticed a familiar face about two tables away. It was Klein! And with his back to us was Riley Morgan. "Don't look now," I said to Janice.

"What is it, Rich?"

"Shh," I said, and listened carefully. Riley was talking.

"Dick," he was saying to Klein, "you can't be serious." I smiled. That's all I heard, but I'm sure they were discussing the negative aspects of hiring me. Every once in a while they'd both shake their heads. If we had been served more quickly we might have been able to duck out undetected. Klein and Morgan stood to leave. I stared straight ahead, ignoring them, but it was hopeless. They had to walk right by us. Klein spotted me.

"Dick!" he said. "Welcome to Chicago." Riley left and Klein and I had our interview right there. He began again with his idea that the Bulls were just a half player away from a championship. For a couple of hours he tried to sell me on the job. If Morgan had been trying to talk him out of hiring me, Klein didn't let on. Once he's committed to something, his pride won't allow him to change his mind. And he wouldn't allow *me* to change his mind either. I responded negatively to most everything he said. He knew if he asked me right then and there that I would have turned him down flat.

At about 12:30, Janice could hardly stay awake. She begged off and went to bed, but I sat up with Klein for another two and a half hours. By the time I was ready to go to bed, fatigue had moved me more to Klein's side of things. I was in no way ready to say yes, I'll coach the Bulls. But I was more neutral than negative. The difference was hardly noticeable to me, but I'm sure salesman Klein sensed it and went for the jugular. "We've already discussed most of what we were going to in the morning. Would you like to see a baseball game?"

That sounded great. I hadn't ever seen a big league game, and I wanted to have something to remember from this trip to Chicago. He picked me up at 11 that morning and drove me to Northbrook, a northern suburb. I realized that I wasn't going to see the Cubs or the White Sox. We spent the whole afternoon watching some high school kids play ball. It was one of those interminable games that just keeps dragging out until even the substitutes are tired of it. It was terrible. After the game Klein told me that we could have some free time to shop around in Evanston. "I'll pick you up for dinner at eight o'clock." he said.

We hadn't planned to do any shopping, so Janice and I walked the streets of Evanston some more. Klein had been promising some real incentives, and I was discussing them with her. "I just don't think I want any part of this," I said.

Klein took us to dinner in Glenview. Five or six different people said hello to him and he introduced us to each as the Johnsons. I could tell by the looks on their faces that they weren't buying it. At first they thought, I'll bet that's the guy the Bulls are interviewing for the coaching job. Then they'd look a little more closely. As they walked away they would shake their heads. I'm sure they were deciding that the Bulls would never hire that crewcut, little guy.

Klein wanted us to have a drink. Janice doesn't drink at all, and I don't drink when she's with me. (And not much when she isn't.) "Janice," Klein said, "will you have a glass of champagne with me when we win the world's championship?"

"Probably not," she said. She wouldn't drink for 20 million dollars. Not even after a championship. (Someday I hope we win one so she'll have to prove that.)

I've never been subtle. My frankness has gotten me into all kinds of trouble, but it's the only way I know how to be. I don't appreciate people who play games. I like everything up front. Klein and I had said just about all that could have been said about the job, the offer, conditions, and all the rest. I was a little tired of it. I wanted some straight and final answers and I wanted to go home. I looked him straight in the eye, and by the tone of my voice, he knew I meant business.

"All right," I said, "what if I come here and turn this franchise around and do the job?" I knew I couldn't, but since he seemed to think I could, I figured I might as well be bargaining from a tough position.

"Well," he said, "in two or three years I'm not going to want to be general manager. I promise you if you come and turn things around and have a winning season, the day you get the club over .500, I'll make you general manager *and* coach. And when you get tired of being general manager, I'll make you a vice-president and part owner."

Now the adrenalin was flowing. My mind had flip-flopped. Here was a possible future. I needed just one more vote of confidence. "What if I get before Bob Boozer and Jerry Sloan and realize that I can't do it?" I don't know what I wanted him to say. Maybe I wanted him to say, Ridiculous, of course you can do it. But he didn't say that.

"Then you just fold up your tent one night and steal away," he said. "If you don't feel 100 per cent that you can handle it, don't take the job." His answer left me cold. He was challenging me. Playing on my pride. I looked deep within myself and I saw myself stealing away in the night, admitting failure.

"I don't feel good about it," I said.

"Fine," Klein said. I had turned down the job.

"Great," I said. "Good night, we've had a nice time." I felt wonderful. The next day we were supposed to watch another baseball game in Northbrook and then leave on Sunday. I saw no reason to stay.

"Could we change our reservations and leave tomorrow morning?" I asked.

"Sure. Whenever you want to leave."

Janice and I slept like babies that night, knowing we had made the right decision. On the way to the airport the next day, Klein made one final push. "You're making a terrible mistake," he said. "You'll regret this. If you don't coach for me now, you'll coach for me someday."

I asked him who he'd get to coach the Bulls now. I was surprised at his answer. I knew I could do a better job. If he hadn't told me, I'd have forgotten the whole experience. "If you change your mind by next Friday, the job is still open."

On the plane I said to Janice, "I sure hope I did the right thing." In the back of my mind I hung on to the fact that I still really had six days in case something unforeseen came up.

At the office the next week I began to realize that I had done just about all I could do at Weber. If I left, Phil could handle the job, and he'd have some good material to work with. The NCAA berth was always a possibility, as long as the Wildcats kept winning. There was a new athletic director, an ok guy, but not one I was used to. Then I'd go home and see my house and realize that I couldn't leave. I couldn't ask Janice to do that.

On Tuesday I got a call from a kid I had been recruiting hard for several years. "Coach, I've decided to go to Brigham Young University." That depressed me. The BYU coaches hadn't even been to his home. It was simply a bigger, nicer school. Just more evidence that Weber State would always be considered the fourth most desirable school in Utah to the scholarship athletes. It made little difference how well our teams fared. We would always be number four. That bothered me daily.

The next day, I got a memo from the department head. It wasn't about anything important, but it was the first time I had ever had a colleague *write* a message to me. I crumpled it up and banked it into my wastebasket. A perfect shot. Then I called Dick Klein.

"You still need a coach?" I asked him.

"Yep."

"I'm your man. What happens next?"

"I'd like to announce it at a press conference a week from tomorrow," he said. "Can you make it?"

"I'll be there," I said.

Janice was like the Rock of Gilbraltar. I said, "Hey, put the house up for sale. We're going to Chicago. I've taken the job." She never missed a beat. I could change jobs once a year and live in any part of the world and she'd be happy.

I went alone to Chicago the day before the press conference. They put me in the same room of the same hotel as my previous visit and put me on pretty much the same schedule. I had nothing to do. They should have entertained me or something. But it was hands off. I was on my own until the next morning when Klein was to pick me up and take me to the Bulls' offices for the press conference. Here I had accepted the job and had never been to the offices. With an afternoon and an evening to kill, I went for a walk.

By now the Northwestern campus was familiar to me. A walk in Evanston, Ill., is nothing like a walk in Utah. The sky grew suddenly dark and the wind developed a bite. It looked like rain. I headed back to my room. From the ninth floor window I could see the clouds rolling in. I flipped on the television. Tornado warnings were out. I had never heard of tornado warnings. It was kind of exciting. I had come all the way to Chicago to see my first tornado. I kept my eyes peeled on the sky, but no tornadoes came.

By dinner time I was bored and depressed. For the first time since I had called Klein, I was sorry I had taken the job. *I might as well make the best of it,* I told myself. *Being a failure in the pros could lead to a better university job than being a success at Weber State.* I decided to look at that side of it from then on. I would fulfill my two-year contract and go for a good job at a major school.

The next morning Klein introduced me to the Chicago press. It was an unusually large press conference because word had leaked out and many curiosity seekers just *had* to see the new nobody. Klein had prepared a little speech. "I would like to introduce my coach," he said. "He's Dick Motta from Weber State College in Ogden, Utah. Some of you may not have heard of him, but he's a winner. In our quest to bring a better team and a world's championship to Chicago, we have decided to go with a winner as the coach.

"We've checked him out very thoroughly. From the junior high to high school and college levels of basketball his teams have won over 80 percent of their games. When you have a toothache, you go to the dentist. When you're sick, you go to the doctor. When you have a losing team, you go to a winner. We have a losing team. And we have gone to a winner. Dick Motta."

I stepped to the microphone and the questions started. "Are you going to be a rubber stamp coach?" I wasn't sure what that meant, but it didn't sound good.

"I'll not be anybody's rubber stamp," I said.

"Are you aware of the poor records of college coaches in the NBA?"

"No."

"Would you like to know?"

"No."

Bill Gleason of the *Sun-Times* said, "You're from Utah?"

"Yes."

"Mormon?"

"Yes."

"How many blacks did you have on your team last year?"

"Five."

"How many did you start?"

"Three."

"Doesn't your religious philosophy degrade blacks?"

"I don't know. I don't think so. I don't study it that much."

Other questions were fired at me but I ignored them. "What difference does it make how many blacks I played last year," I said. I was totally aware that the majority of the players in the NBA are black. And I said that I judge a man on his talent, teamwork, and attitude. "I don't see color on the court." I meant it. There *is* some sort of a limitation about blacks in the Mormon faith. I don't understand it all, but whatever it means, I don't agree with it if it implies that blacks are some how of less intrinsic value than whites.

Gleason listened to the rest of the press conference

and I think he liked me. He whispered to me, "If you coach and act like you spoke today, there's no way you'll succeed in Chicago under the present structure." I had not enjoyed the press conference, and I had especially not liked what I had heard about the records of other college coaches in the NBA.

Then everyone with a camera or a tape recorder wanted a personal interview. I was asked to put on a Bulls' warmup jacket and hold a basketball. I wish I hadn't. Never before in my career had I allowed anyone to take a gimmick photo of me. I don't use gimmicks in my coaching, and I don't like to use gimmicks for the press. The picture of me wearing that jacket and grinning went all over the country, and I really regretted it.

I got the impression from the press that they were basketball fans who wanted to see the franchise stay in Chicago. They could have torn me to shreds for the direct way I had talked at the conference, and they could have nailed Klein for hiring *Dick Who from Weber Where?* But they didn't. They took what seemed to be a genuine wait-and-see attitude. I appreciated that, and while I don't believe the Chicago papers have assigned the most knowledgeable basketball writers to the Bulls, they haven't hurt us much. Moving from the basketball beat to any of the other big league teams is considered a promotion in Chicago.

I felt low on my way back to Utah, mostly because the reporters seemed to think that the personalities in the Bulls' front office would make the situation impossible for me. Besides, there wasn't much talent on the ballclub, they said. One of the writers told me later that he had expected a mild-mannered, putty type of coach who would be a rubber stamp while Klein would be the team spokesman. He didn't like that idea, but he said that type of man would probably get along better with Klein than I would. They were right, as I would discover.

The news had broken by the time I got back to Ogden. The neighborhood, the college, the team, everyone was shocked. A little neighbor boy came to the door the next day. "Hey coach," he said, "Is it true that you're gonna coach in Chicago?"

"Yup."

"Is that in the NBA?"

"It sure is."

"Are you gonna play against a lot of good teams?" That hit me hard.

"I don't know. I guess we are," I said. The thought scared me a bit.

"You gonna play against Bill Russell?"

"Yeah."

"Will you get his autograph and send it to me?"

"Are you kidding?" I said. "I'll get his autograph, but I'm gonna keep it!"

Day after day after day after day for the next two months I went over in my mind what I would say to the professional giants who made up the Chicago Bulls. Would they respect me? Would I know enough basketball so that they could have confidence in me? I was almost paranoid. I hadn't played after my junior year of high school. I wasn't sure I looked forward to my first head to head meeting with the big, bad, rough, tough NBA pros. Maybe I would realize after the first practice that it was tent-packing and away-stealing time.

From the day I had been cut from the high school

basketball team I had had trouble trusting people. I couldn't read them. I knew it wouldn't do me any good to distrust everyone, but I wanted an easy, uncomplicated system. No games. I had decided to trust any person I could look in the eye and shake hands with. Until he crossed me, I would be naive and assume that his intentions were as good as mine. I was trusting Dick Klein. I believed that he would produce video tapes of every team in the league and a typewritten report on every player as he had promised.

CHAPTER **6**

CHICAGO

WE SPENT FOUR DAYS driving to Chicago since we couldn't cover too many miles at a stretch with three young children. I'm not much for traveling, especially by car, but I forced myself to take it easy, and we made a vacation of it. We hit all the scenic views and stopped at museums and parks. In spite of myself, I enjoyed it.

Riley Morgan found us a home to rent for a few months while I got acquainted with the front office and Janice went house hunting. I took the elevated train to the Bulls' offices so she could have the car, and I quickly felt like a Chicagoan. I never did get used to the weather and the wind and the lack of scenery, but living in Chicago was a small price to pay for a job with the potential mine had.

I told Janice to find any home she wanted in our price range but to make sure it didn't have too big a yard. If I wanted to raise a yard I would have stayed on the farm. I liked the house she chose in Northbrook, and we were lucky to get into a good neighborhood. I'm not a very good neighbor because I like to keep to myself. Janice makes up for that. The neighbors respect my job and my privacy, and they're good basketball fans. They come to a lot of the games.

In about a month I would be meeting the rookies at training camp. I hadn't had anything to do with the player draft, so all I could do was hope that Klein had done a good job. I didn't know anything about the offensive trends in the NBA, what would work and what wouldn't. It was beginning to worry me. Should I try the stuff I used at Weber? Would it work against the 100 per cent man-to-man defenses? The no-zone defense rule was about all I knew about the NBA. I got myself a rule book and studied it daily. And I badgered Klein about the video tapes of each team he had promised. I desperately needed information on the rest of the league.

Every day I got a different excuse. "They're not here yet, but they're coming." I wanted to see what the options were and maybe devise my own offense. But I had nothing to go by. And August 18 approached. Each day at noon I was to join Klein for lunch at a big round table in a loop restaurant. There, before various audiences of from three to seven friends, he would expound on the trends in the NBA. I wasn't impressed, but I was listening. I would have listened to the cleaning lady if she said she had any info on the NBA.

I began to get wary of the whole operation when I noticed that the phones in the office were hardly ringing off the wall. We had more calls for tickets at Weber State than the Bulls seemed to be getting. The whole office was run pretty shoddily. I was worried. There wasn't much promotion or advance sales. And the office was on the twelfth floor of a downtown office building. I thought an NBA club should have some romance, a street level, storefront type of operation with a banner or signs letting fans know how and where to get tickets.

I felt I knew enough basketball to get a feeling for the league by seeing a film of each team in action, but days passed and they didn't come. I finally realized that they weren't coming at all. Had I known that I would not get to see the films I'd never have taken the job. I put pressure on Klein. I was tired of the long lunches, and I needed some information.

Klein introduced me to his scout, Jerry Krause. Krause had scouted for Baltimore and was also working for the Cleveland baseball Indians of the American League. He didn't have a whole lot of time, so Klein had him meet me at the office one morning at 10 o'clock. I hoped I would at least get something to go on.

In the NBA a scout doesn't usually watch the other pro teams. You play them often enough during the year that scouting is generally unnecessary. Unless there's a coach or a team in the league you have not seen before, your scout sticks to watching 150 or so college games and knowing who should be drafted. So Krause hadn't seen an abundance of pro games recently. But he wouldn't admit that to me.

When I met him, I got the impression that he was afraid I might bring in someone new to scout, maybe an old friend. Krause came on strong. At the end of an hour I had had enough.

He told me so much meaningless trivia about NBA players that I was bored out of my mind. And a little too much of his conversation was about his own qualifications. He had an over knowledge of the players. He knew things about them he didn't need to know.

Then he got onto the fact that he had been personally responsible for making Gus Johnson the great Baltimore star that he was. My Weber team had faced Johnson five times in one year, and I felt he was one of the two best I had ever seen. For once I was glad to have the daily luncheon appointment with Klein. It gave me a reason to get away from Krause. Almost. He joined us for lunch and the monologue continued. If this was the front office, the whole franchise must be shaky, I decided. Was I hired because they felt that I would fit in?

Finally August 18 arrived. And so did the rookies. Dave Newmark of Columbia and Tom Boerwinkle of Tennessee were my rookie centers. Both were seven-footers and white. I had a vague problem with the fact that with all the great black centers in the nation that year, this one team had wound up with two white ones. Jerry Krause thought he was going to help me out. He showed up at Lake Forest. "I'm going to move into training camp with Tom Boerwinkle and teach him everything he needs to know about being an NBA center." He went on and on, telling me how quickly Tom would learn under his guidance. I was seething. Finally, I had simply had it. I was out of patience and courtesy. I spoke very clearly and directly. He could not misunderstand.

"Jerry, you are not my assistant coach. You are not moving in with Tom Boerwinkle. I do not want you to attend any practices. You are not welcome to be around me or to call me any more. I don't know what kind of job I'm going to do in Chicago, but I'm going to be damn sure it's my job and no one else's."

I didn't enjoy doing that. In fact I felt a little dirty afterward. But I knew time would heal it. He was hurt, sure. But I had no choice. Things would have been worse if I hadn't confronted him. He stayed away . . . for awhile.

There wasn't a *good* basketball player in the rookie camp, and I mean that sincerely. I was afraid that I might have been expecting too much from potential pros. Three of the rookies had been signed to the roster, and while I respect all of them as people, I would not sign them if they tried out for me today. Dave Newmark, Tom Boerwinkle, and Lloyd Peterson out of Oregon State, were already locked in to no-cut contracts. (Boerwinkle has since improved tremendously, of course, and is an asset to the Bulls, so at least something good came from that first training camp.)

I invited Phil to help me out at rookie camp. He was glad to get a peek at what the NBA was all about. We opened the practices to the public and had 30-40 spectators each day for our double two-hour sessions. I noticed a couple of guys in the stands who looked familiar, but I didn't find out until later that they were Jerry Sloan and Flynn Robinson. Jerry had driven up from his home in Evansville, Ind., to see the new coach. He is the only Bull left from the original expansion team of 1966.

When I met Sloan, the first thing I asked him was, "Is this a .500 ball club?" Ringing in my ears were the promises of Klein that if I got the team to .500, we'd make the playoffs every year, I'd be general manager, Mr. Basketball in Chicago, vice-president, part owner, a wealthy man. Sloan had his doubts.

"Maybe if it gets turned around to the right direction," he said.

Dr. Bob Biel, a Chicago Heights podiatrist, had been hired to be the trainer for the two weeks of rookie camp until the regular trainer was free to join us. I could tell right away that Biel was a class guy. I didn't know that he had been responsible for Sloan's early visit to the camp. I found later that he had been impressed by my schedules, my lesson plans. I had the rookies running drills to the minute, and their tails were dragging.

Biel called Sloan after a few days of that and told him, "You'd better be ready. You'd better get here early and you'd better come in shape, 'cause this guy'll kill you."

That was what Sloan wanted to hear. I was to learn that Jerry was a glutton for punishment. He's from the old school where the athlete believes that he improves in direct proportion to the torture he forces upon his body. You can't work him hard enough. He pushes all the time. In practice games he'll dive for loose balls, play his man tight, and scrap every second, ignoring fatigue. Sloan liked what he saw in rookie camp. He actually looked forward to my rough workouts.

Other Bulls began to filter in as the rookie camp wore on. They would come down during breaks and introduce themselves. The rookie camp was much too long, but it was the best thing that could have happened to me. The veterans got a chance to see how I worked. They knew when they finally took the court that I would not tolerate any loafing. They knew I was serious, and that I cared only about developing a winning team. I think I sold myself to them before our first formal meeting.

In September the veterans joined us, all but three holdouts: Bob Boozer, Flynn Robinson, and Keith Erickson. Jimmy Washington, Clem Haskins, Jim "Bad News" Barnes, Barry Clemens, and Sloan made up the balance of the veterans. After the first regular day of training camp, Robinson came to terms with Klein and joined us. The next day, Boozer was aboard too. I was glad. I thought holdouts would hurt us, especially since I was trying to teach these guys my system.

Despite the fact that I hadn't seen any of the films Klein had promised, we were communicating well. He seemed to appreciate me, and I was getting a little more enthused because the ballplayers were responding and cooperating. The only problem with Keith Erickson. He was still in California.

I wanted him. I looked forward to coaching him. The players, to a man, liked him and respected his ability. I had seen him play in college and I thought he would be a key man for us. I don't mind saying that if we had had Erickson for the 1973-74 season we would have had a shot at the championship, barring injuries. It would have freed me to put Sloan at forward when I rested Chet Walker. Some of the 1968-69 players felt that if we had Erickson, his team attitude alone would contribute to our making the playoffs.

Every day after practice I asked Klein how things were coming with Erickson. "It looks like he's going to be a hard sign," he'd say, "but we'll get him." Our first exhibition game was approaching. We were to play Baltimore in Washington, D.C. Even if we got

Erickson, he would be too late to learn my system before that, but I wanted to be able to quit worrying about him before the exhibition season got underway.

The Wednesday before the Baltimore game Klein took three calls in my room from the Los Angeles Lakers. When Klein got off the phone he told me, "They want him real bad. They'll pay big money too. I'll sign him if I can, but it doesn't look too good now."

I told him I'd sure hate to see Keith go to Los Angeles, already the toughest team in our division. "We can get some good players for him," Klein assured me. "Baltimore wants him and they're talking about giving up Jack Marin or Gus Johnson."

I didn't know anything about Marin, but I believed Klein. If he put him in the same category with Gus Johnson, then both of them were better than Erickson. I couldn't imagine Baltimore really giving up Johnson, even for Keith Erickson. I didn't care too much who we got for Erickson. All I knew was that I didn't want to wind up playing against Keith in our own division.

"One thing I won't do," Klein promised, "is trade him to Los Angeles."

As we walked down to dinner we passed Barry Clemens and Jerry Sloan in the hallway. Jerry was characteristically direct. "What's happening with Erickson?" he asked.

"I'm having trouble, Jerry," Klein said. "May not get him signed. We'll make a trade."

"I hear Los Angeles wants him," Sloan said.

"We'll never trade him to Los Angeles," Klein said. It was reassuring to hear him say it again.

The veterans took to me right away, which really

made my job easier. We kidded each other a lot. They often came up to me with the news that I had been traded, or that the whole team had been traded, or that we had changed our team mascot, or whatever they thought was funny. When Barry Clemens told me the day before the Baltimore game (the very morning after my discussion with Klein about Erickson) that Keith had been traded to Los Angeles for Erwin Mueller, I laughed. What a card. Mueller had been with the Bulls two years before but had been traded when the fans started booing him. I knew Klein wouldn't trade Erickson for Mueller. The morning practice went well and I thought we looked pretty good, with the first exhibition game approaching. At lunch I got a call from a sportswriter. "What about the trade?" he said.

"What trade is that, John?" I said.

"Mueller for Erickson."

"You gotta be kiddin'."

"No," he said. "That's the truth. It happened to-day."

Clemens hadn't been putting me on. The blood drained from my face. It wasn't so much that we had gotten gypped, which we had, but Klein had promised that he wouldn't trade Erickson to a team within our division, Los Angeles in particular.

I had been enjoying myself up to that second. I hung up and called Klein. "What the hell is going on around here?" I said. "You make a trade you promised you wouldn't make. It's a bad one. And on top of that my players know about it four hours before I do, and even then I don't hear it from you."

"I had to make the deal," he said. "I just had to."

"Well, I want you to know that you couldn't have

hurt me personally any more than you have. I just hope you realize what you've done." I hung up. He had traded a player without telling me. I knew exactly what he thought of me. He had clearly established my role. There was never a cordial word between us again. I had been sincere in my coaching. I had been willing to give my all. I hadn't asked to see player contracts, I hadn't asked to be in on the details. But I did want to feel trusted, included, consulted. I decided right then that I would quit at the end of the season. I couldn't imagine anything changing my mind.

I was dead inside. It was as if I had been told I had cancer and had three months to live. I like Erwin Mueller, and I'd like to have him on my team again, but for some reason the Chicago fans got down on him, and a man just can't play when he's getting booed by the home crowd. Anyway, a week before the infamous trade, Klein had told me that Mueller was one of the worst players he'd had in Chicago.

Later Thursday afternoon, Klein called me back. "Mueller will be arriving at the airport tomorrow morning at the same time you guys are leaving for Washington. You can take him with you."

"There's no need of his going with us, so maybe it'd be better for him to come here to Lake Forest and get in shape," I said.

"Why don't you want him to go?" Klein said. "You could get to know him a little."

"He doesn't know my offense and he doesn't have any idea of what we're trying to do defensively."

"Oh, that's ok. Put him on the bench next to you for the first half and he can pick it up by half time." That was the ultimate insult. Few offenses are simple enough for even the best players to pick up by half-time. And mine was the product of years of development. I had thrown myself into the job, especially after it had become apparent that I would not have the aid of any films of the opponents. I was completely dedicated, my whole purpose in life was to make winners of the Chicago Bulls. I knew nothing else and nothing else interested me. To have Klein refer to my system as if it were a junior high chalk talk was almost more than I could take. We became like icebergs.

I rammed myself back into the shell I had created as a senior in high school. It became impossible for me to trust strangers. If someone patted me on the back and told me I was doing a good job, I thought only of Klein and said, "Yeah, sure."

I was a good boy. I took Mueller with me, but I didn't play him. Strangely, I would come to like Erwin. I didn't take the fiasco out on him. He played well for me. The fans hadn't forgotten him though and midway through the season he would beg to be traded. The boos kept coming. Klein had told me that Mueller had intentionally thrown bad passes in an effort to get traded two years before. I don't believe that, but if Klein really thought so, why would he have traded Erickson for him? I'll never know.

For some reason the guys on the team decided to give me a chance to succeed or fail without any hassle. Coaching Jerry Sloan and learning how much he would give of himself was a real pleasure. Bob Boozer, a real pro, accepted everything I said and really hustled for me. I grew to respect him. I shudder to think what that first year would have been like without Bob in the lineup.

During the exhibition season I really raped the player's intelligence. I used them. I asked them questions about every phase of the game from defense to rules. It was like a father-son relationship, and often I felt like the son. They carried me, advised me, helped me. And when I said move, they moved.

Barry Clemens proved to be invaluable to me during that first season. Barry was my third forward, a super intellect. I found him to be a genuine, class type guy. He stuttered, but he got the words out when he needed them. He sat next to me most of the time, and his photographic memory came in handy. Barry could remember how many fouls each guy had committed, how many points each had scored, even how many shots had been taken. Once at half time he read the stat sheet and came to me. "C-C-Coach," he said, "They've g-got me d-down for one too many sh-shots. They m-must have c-counted the desperation shot." It was uncanny. He even told me the spots on the floor from which he had taken every shot. He wanted me to succeed and most of all he wanted the team to succeed. He was always ready because he prepared mentally for each game.

My first ever NBA regular season game was against the Knicks in Madison Square Garden. I'd have been thrilled to have lost there, but winning my debut before 19,500 opposing fans was a real kick. New York is the basketball capital of the world. Every coach at every level dreams of taking his team there. I still love playing in the Garden, and my teams have done well there. Clem Haskins hit a clutch basket for us with just a few minutes to go and we won by four. I raised my fist and jumped around like a cheerleader. Bob Boozer grabbed me in the locker room and swung me around. I still act that way after big or close wins. The day I lose my enthusiasm, I'm getting out.

The reporters crowded around and commented that it was just like a college atmosphere. One said, "We expected to see some little hick, but even your clothes are in style."

Another said, "This has got to be the most important game in your career." I thought quickly, *Wow, that's not true!*

"No," I said.

"What could be more important than this?" My answer was quoted all over the country.

"My Grace High School team winning the state basketball championship in Idaho." I can't visualize anything taking the place of that. I would imagine that if the Bulls ever win the world's championship, I'll be so numb I won't be able to compare it with that first thrill. (I see Chet Walker's diamond championship ring, and I want one. Bad.)

I loved the excitement of winning the opener, especially on the road. The next night we beat Milwaukee, also on the road. I said to myself, *The big, bad NBA isn't that tough.* I told Janice, "Our kids are playing pretty well. We're not a great team, but from what I've seen so far, we can compete. It's not so hard to win in this league."

Two games later we were at .500 and we didn't see an even win-loss column again for three years. Our home opener was against Bill Russell and the Boston Celtics. It was Bill's last year in the league and I'm glad I got to the NBA soon enough to have competed against him. I had never seen him before except on television. It was like a fairy tale, a dream come true. How many coaches of small college teams would give their life savings for my job?

While the team was getting used to my offense (I base it around six stock plays which can have as many as two dozen variations each), I decided to go with the best defensive team I could put on the floor. We weren't scoring exceptionally, so I was concerned that we play a sticky defense.

Clem Haskins, Sloan, and Flynn Robinson were my guards. Flynn was probably the best shooter and most flashy player, but he was the least proficient defensive man of the three. I started the other two, to the puzzlement of many fans, writers, and Flynn. He had scored over 42 points in a playoff victory against the Lakers the year before and had received a nice raise. I tried my best to sell him on the idea that third guard would be his best role. The backup players, at least the third guard and third forward, are very key people. I wanted him to come in when we were down, or when we were flat, and open things up with his shooting. He didn't buy it. He wasn't happy on the bench, and that's bad for a third guard.

I was building, and Flynn wasn't cooperating. I was playing rookie centers with Mueller backing them up because I knew the future of the franchise depended on them (and because they were all I had). I wanted a third guard who could identify with his role and excel at it. I told Klein I wanted Robinson traded. "I can't trade him," Klein said. "He's the best guard prospect in the league."

I let it ride for a few more games, but by mid-November I knew it was hopeless. I needed a playmaking type guard. Robinson wasn't fitting in. Klein didn't seem to want to budge. At nine o'clock one Friday night I called him. "You've got to get rid of Flynn," I said.

"I can't do it," he said. "He's too good a player." I couldn't believe he had refused. Who was coaching this team, anyway? I hadn't asked to see salaries or contracts. I didn't even want to help in the player draft after not having seen any college games. I just wanted to be heard when I said that a player didn't fit in my system. I thought it was little to ask of the general manager. The next morning I called Klein again. I had reached a decision and I was serious.

"Mr. Klein," I began, "I don't want Flynn Robinson on my team any more. You have a choice and it's a very clear cut choice. There's a game tonight. If Flynn Robinson is in the dressing room when I get there, I'm leaving. Trade him today or I won't be there."

At two o'clock that afternoon the phone rang. Klein sounded depressed. "Well, Flynn's gone," he said.

"Great, who'd you get?"

"Well, we got Bobby Weiss from Milwaukee."

"Is he good?"

"Yeah. He's a left-handed guard. If we make the trade we've got to take another guy too. Bob Love."

"We get two players for Flynn?" I asked. "What does this Love guy do?"

"I don't know," he said. "Nothing. He can't do anything. I gave Weiss your number so he'll probably be calling. I've made the trade and I hope you're satisfied, you big boob." And he hung up.

Satisfied? I was elated. Had I any idea of what those two players would mean to the Bulls in future years I'd have jumped for joy. When Weiss called he said he was happy to be with the Bulls and that he thought I'd like Bob Love. "He's a good, hard worker and I think he'll be an asset."

I made a mistake that night though. I told Weiss to get a hold of Love and get to Chicago in time for the game. We had one of our typical crowds that night, around 650. I introduced Love and Weiss as the players we got in the Flynn Robinson trade. I learned a lesson. Robinson had been popular in Chicago, so his replacements were booed. The next time I traded a player in mid-season, I let the new man make his debut on the road. That way the home fans would have read about him before he played in the Stadium.

We had sold only 38 season tickets that year and it was depressing to play in the vacuum. We can stuff 19,500 into the Chicago Stadium, so less than a thousand fans hardly pay for the heat and light. We looked forward to playing on the road because, since we were one of the weaker teams in the league, our games were usually preliminaries to better games in an NBA doubleheader. When we had single games the opposing management had to throw gigantic promotional giveaways to get people to come out. I got dozens of free hats, shirts, basketballs, and autographed pictures that year. (That's the bad thing about winning now. We don't get in on all the free souvenirs!)

Boozer and Jimmy Washington were playing a lot of forward for me and the two rookie centers were trading off. Tom would come a long way, but at that time he was very much a rookie. They both were, and we took a beating at center. Often I had to have Mueller back them up. He wasn't nearly as tall as Tom or Dave, but at 6-8 he was big enough. And he hustled. He was a good passer and smart. Out of desperation I was almost to the point where I had to start him. The fans were still booing him, and he asked to be traded. I told him we'd have to get someone decent in return. "I've got to have someone who can at least do the job he's doing," I told Klein.

Klein agreed. "I'll work out the best deal I can for him," he said.

I'm not sure why Klein didn't just let me quit when I hit him with the Flynn Robinson ultimatum. I guess he had committed himself to me in front of the other owners and couldn't admit that he'd made a mistake. Now it seemed he was trying to be cooperative on the Mueller problem too. Maybe things were looking up. Or maybe he had realized that I was not going to be just a follower. I didn't know.

Just before the trading deadline Mueller did a great job against Nate Thurmond in San Francisco, and we won. Klein had been telling me, "We're going to trade him, but we'd better get something out of it." After that game we flew home, coach-class as usual. An all-night flight. (Young franchises pinch pennies, but we were probably the cheapest traveling team in the league. First-class seats aren't really big enough for professional basketball players, let alone coach.)

I got home at seven o'clock. "Dick Klein called while you were in flight," Janice said. "Mueller has been sold to Seattle."

"Sold?" I said. "What did we get in return?"

"Just money, I guess," Janice said. She guessed right.

I knew Klein wouldn't be up yet, so I waited until 9:30 and called him at his house. "You really sold Mueller to Seattle?" I said.

"Yes," he said, and told me the figure.

"Listen, we've got to get together," I said. "Soon." The Bulls had a road trip to Philadelphia the next day, and Klein was busy, so we scheduled a meeting for when we got back.

A Philadelphia writer asked me what I thought of the Mueller deal. "Erwin wasn't a great player," I said. "But he was someone we could use and we're going to miss him. I'd like to throw a dollar bill out on the floor and see if it can play in his place."

I got the feeling from reading the papers that Klein was in some sort of trouble with the other Bull owners. It was no secret that I wasn't happy. I was ready to quit. And this time, as during the Flynn flareup, I would have. I asked our publicity man, Ben Bentley, to join me in my meeting with Klein. I wanted a witness. I felt I had been lied to once too often, and I wanted assurance that it wouldn't happen again.

Somehow word got out to the media that the meeting was for more than just chitchat. When I arrived to see Klein, reporters crowded around. Bentley was a little late. I told Klein that I preferred to wait for Ben. "I'll not meet with you without a witness," I said. He knew something was up.

When Ben arrived we really went at it. "This is it, Dick," I said. "I'm leaving." I told him I couldn't work under the present structure where trades were made behind my back and where good ballplayers were being sold at the expense of the club.

"I don't want you to leave," Klein said. "You've gotta stay out the year." I had been advised that my contract had loopholes, so I insisted that it be changed. The way it read, I was under a "personal services" retainer. In other words, I could have been made into a ticket seller with no recourse. I had him change the contract to stipulate that coaching was my only responsibility, and that there would be no more trades without my knowledge. He consented.

I decided that I wasn't going to walk away from the battle. I felt I was fairly qualified in the league. The next time Klein hassled me, I asked Benny to witness the conversation again. "If you don't like the way I do my job," I said, "fire me."

"I wouldn't give you the satisfaction," Klein said. That was all I needed to hear. I wanted to build a winner as fast as I could and make the Bulls a contender in spite of everything. I had my love for the game, a dream job (considering), and all the motivation I needed. If Klein wanted me out, he was going to have to fire me.

CHAPTER **7**

CHANGE

BOB WEISS MOVED RIGHT IN and did a fine job at third guard for us. I guess I proved how important that position is to me (and how much action a good third guard will see) when I played Weiss in every game for five years until a foot injury sidelined him late in the 1973-74 season. As our "sixth" man and a seldom starter, Bob has had the fifth highest total of minutes played for the Bulls for the last several seasons.

I wasn't as impressed with Bob Love those first few months he was with us during 1968-69, although he hustled in practice and seemed to have a pretty shot. His jumping ability had been impaired by an operation two years before, and I didn't find too many opportunities to get him into the lineup. Just about the time he was showing the most promise, and when he probably could have done us the most good, he was in an automobile accident. He snapped back from a shoulder injury in about three weeks, but I was unable to play him much the rest of the season. Of course, he was to become a very important part of the Bulls in following years.

We didn't have much fun during my first season. Except when we played the expansion teams, Milwaukee and Phoenix, we went into every game as underdogs. On paper we were the weaker team. There were seven teams in our division, and four would make the playoffs. Phoenix was the weak sister and wound up with just 17 wins, and Detroit had a rough year under a new coach, too. They were in sixth place, and we trailed San Diego by a half game for the fourth playoff berth going into the fourth to the last game of the regular season.

We were playing Los Angeles in Chicago and we drew a crowd of about 3,000 (not bad for those early years). A loss would put us out of the running for the playoffs. The game was tight to the end. With four seconds to play we had the ball and trailed 93-92. We missed what would have been the game winning shot. Tom Boerwinkle roared up to yank down the rebound. There was not time to call a timeout or to pass off. Big Tom went back up with the ball. He was fouled by Jerry West and went to the free throw line with no time showing on the clock. He had three chances to make two shots. If he makes just one, the game goes into overtime. Two and we win. Miss all three and we can forget the playoffs.

The first shot went right in the hole, whirled around

and flew out. I saw the blood drain from Tom's face. He hadn't considered the possibility of missing all three until that first one. It was as if someone had plucked the ball out before it got through the net. I didn't want to watch the second shot. I turned around to get a drink of water. I heard the crowd groan and turned back in time to see the ball fall short. *Oh, come on, Tom. Just make one.*

Missing three straight foul shots is called a turkey or the hat trick everywhere in the NBA. Tom pulled it off. He overcompensated on the last shot and bounced it hard off the board. He was just sick about it, but it happens to the best of players. You're not really a pro until you've bagged a turkey.

We finished the season with the knowledge that we had no chance to make the playoffs. We had won 33 games, tying the club record which had been set two years before. The Bulls had won just 27 the previous year, but they had made the playoffs. My first season was the first and only time Chicago didn't make the playoffs.

I had been used to winning. I lost almost as many games that year as I had lost in my entire career before that. We'd have had to lose 16 more games to have tied Phoenix for last place in our division. They got to flip against Milwaukee, who finished last in the other division, for the right to first choice in the college player draft. There was little doubt who would be the first choice. Milwaukee won the toss and picked Lew Alcindor of UCLA. Lew had offers from the Globetrotters, the ABA, and the Bucks. Talk about a player turning a franchise around! Everyone should finish last once.

I had seen some encouraging signs during the season, and I had gained some self confidence about coaching in the NBA. The Seattle coach had quit. I called the general manager out there and asked if he needed a coach. I was willing and anxious to leave, so I didn't worry about seeming forward. Maybe Seattle didn't appreciate my boldness. I was told that they were interested and that they would get back to me. I never heard from them again.

I took the family back to Utah for the summer, and Ben Bentley called frequently to keep me abreast of developments in Chicago. Late in the summer he told me changes were in the works.

"What kind of changes?" I asked. I was only interested in one change.

"There might be a move on to change general managers," Ben said. That was what I wanted to hear. I felt that any change at that post would be good for the Bulls.

A month later we moved back east. I was called in about two weeks before training camp was to begin. "Give us an assessment of the team," the owners said. "What will it take to win? How close are the Bulls to being a playoff team? A contender?"

I answered as honestly as I could, but the meeting puzzled me. I didn't know what they were getting at. I told them that I felt we needed some personnel changes, but that I was also optimistic. Finally the reason for the meeting came out. They wanted to make sure I would have no complaints about their hiring a new general manager. Complaints? They could have hired Satan himself and I would have been happy with the change.

"Have you ever heard of Pat Williams?" they asked. I said no, not remembering that I had met him once during the past season at one of our games against Philadelphia. He was a 29-year-old promotional wizard who had come from the Philadelphia Phillies baseball farm system to become the business manager of the 76ers. In just one year there he had impressed the Bulls' owners. They had him hidden out in Chicago, trying to keep the news from breaking before they announced his hiring. I offered to put him up for the night.

Pat and I sat up talking for several hours. I was really glad to have some new blood in the front office. He seemed eager to help turn things around in Chicago, and he promised to work closely with me on everything connected with player personnel.

"What do you think of Jerry Krause?" I asked him. It was an unfair question. He wasn't really aware of Krause, and could have had no idea of my problems with him.

"He's fine with me," Pat said. "Until he shows me he can't do the job, I'll be happy with him." I was already convinced that Krause wasn't doing the job, and I probably should have told Williams how strongly I felt. But I didn't.

The next day, after Pat's press conference, we announced the trade of Jimmy Washington to Philadelphia for Chet Walker. Pat had engineered the deal and made a name for himself that first day.

The 76ers saw our Washington as the answer to their problems. They felt he was an up and coming superstar, and they were willing to give up Walker for him. It became a dream come true. Walker is a Sloan type, at least in attitude, one of the most coachable guys who's ever played for me. And a real pro besides. Walker was a bargain and a half.

Chet wasn't too excited about the trade at first. He was hurt that the team he had helped win a championship two years before would trade him to a fledgling team like Chicago. Pat and I visited Chet that night in Philadelphia and told him that we thought it would be worth his while to agree to the move, though it meant leaving his home area. I told him that our offense was built around a balanced attack and a good defense. I don't know how convinced he was, but he came, and I think he's happy now that he did. I know I am.

We had our eyes on Bob Kaufman of Seattle, thinking the same of him that Philadelphia thought of Jimmy Washington. The next day we traded Bob Boozer to Seattle for Kaufman. Chicago fans were really beginning to watch the new general manager.

Going into training camp I had already decided on my starting lineup. I'd go with Sloan and Clem Haskins at guards, Walker and Kaufman at the forwards, and Boerwinkle at center. Bob Love would be my third forward, Weiss my third guard. All during training camp I insisted that Kaufman would be my starting forward. I wasn't open to any other options, and I gave no one else a chance. And I learned from that coaching mistake.

By the end of the exhibition season I was beginning to realize that Kaufman wasn't the forward I thought he had been. I was worried. Love had looked good, scoring well and playing excellent defense during the exhibition games, but Kaufman had been groomed for the top job, and I was bound to give him a good shot.

The pressure of the regular season told the story. Kaufman wasn't ready yet to be a starting forward in

the NBA. Going into our fourth game at San Francisco we just weren't clicking. During the pre-game
warmups I called Love aside. "I'm going to start you
tonight," I said. His career since is history. He won
the regular starting job in a matter of games and shot
his average to well over 20 points a game. He played
super defense as well and has started almost every
game for me.

Bob has averaged about 45 minutes a game for the
Bulls. When I think back about the trade of Flynn
Robinson for Love and Weiss, the trade I was called
a *boob* over, I laugh. I feel fortunate to have been in
on one of the greatest trades in the history of the
league. I don't say that lightly. There have been
some super trades in this league. But I didn't initiate
the Robinson trade. I didn't even know the talent
enough to judge it. But it's the best thing that ever
happened to the Bulls.

For Weiss and Love the move to Chicago was a good
one. They left the lowly Bucks for the not quite so
lowly Bulls. For a guy like Chet Walker, the move to
Chicago had to be seen in its perspective to be good.
Chet had played for the 76ers when they had been,
in my opinion, the best pro team ever. I would get a
lot of argument on that, but that Philadelphia club of
1967-68 was something else. When you have a guy
of the calibre of Billy Cunningham playing *third*
forward, you gotta know the team is great. Wilt
Chamberlain was the center, Chet and Luke Jackson
were the forwards, and the 76ers had a lineup of
guards that wouldn't quit, from Hal Greer to Wally
Jones and Matt Goukas.

Chicago was the cesspool of the league. Oh, there
were clubs who lost more games but few treated the

ballplayers with less respect. There is a meal allot-
ment given to the players when they are on the road.
For a coach like me, the money is too much and I'm
able to save half of it or so. But for the players, around
$20 a day is not exorbitant. Remember that these
guys need four large meals every day, especially game
days. But the Chicago Bulls of the late 1960's looked
for ways to dock the players' meal allowances. If the
plane we were on served breakfast (never enough
for an athletic giant), the players had to forfeit their
breakfast money. And sometimes we caught early
flights, just to make sure a meal was included. We
also took a lot of night flights to save money. I encouraged proper rest and nutrition, but the hotels
we stayed in and the airline meals we ate to save
money made me look hypocritical. Luckily, with the
addition of Walker, the improvement (or discovery)
of Bob Love, and the debut of Pat Williams in our
front office, we took on a new look of professionalism
during my second season. So, we survived the cheap
reputation.

I wanted Chet Walker to be our player representa-
tive and Jerry Sloan to be the team captain, so I
asked the players to vote. "This is a democratic
election," I told them. "But I would like to nominate
Walker and Sloan."

"Do we have to vote?" Weiss asked.

"No, not if my choices are all right with you," I
said.

Everybody said, "Yeah," so that was that. It's been
that way every year. If we ever get to the point where
the players *do* want to vote, I'll be sure I count the
ballots. There are about four guys on my current team

who could be good player reps, and if anyone else was nominated, I'd see to it that he is not elected.

We traded our third round draft choice, a playmaker named Norm Van Lier, to Cincinnati for big Walt Wesley. Wesley moved in as our backup center so we could get rid of Dave Newmark who simply wasn't a big league center. Wesley really helped us, and I doubt we would have made the playoffs had it not been for him. And Walker. And Love. And Sloan. And Haskins. It was a good year. An encouraging year. Pat and his zany promotions were an instant hit. Our attendance zoomed over the 10,000 mark, and that had a great impact on the players.

Probably the best thing that happened to us in the 1969-70 season was that we won the first and only protest ever upheld in the NBA. A $1,000 deposit accompanies all protest appeals, and if you lose the appeal, you lose the grand too. Our hassle began with a few seconds to play in a game against the league-leading Atlanta Hawks at the Chicago Stadium.

We were down by two and had the ball. Our desperation shot missed but Tom Boerwinkle tipped it back up and in as the seconds ticked away. Amidst all the screaming and cheering the referees were waving their arms and blowing their whistles. They said the buzzer had sounded before the tip in. But the buzzer hadn't sounded at all! The clock still showed a full second to play!

The refs wouldn't change their decision. I asked the timekeeper if the buzzer had sounded. He said no. I asked him if he had touched the clock since stopping it after the tip in. He said no.

The sportswriters crowded around as Pat turned

on a tape recorder, then turned on the clock. A second passed and the buzzer rang. We had our evidence. The refs had long since left the court. Video taped replays also showed that time had not expired. Pat filed the protest.

The papers played up the story and suddenly loyal Chicago fans were coming out of the woodwork. During the few days before the commissioner's ruling every paper in town ran several stories on the fiasco. We played some rough teams and hosted Milwaukee for Lew Alcindor's pro debut in Chicago. For several games in a row we had record crowds, and the attendance picture at the stadium has been different ever since. The commissioner ruled that the game was to be played over with one second to play.

When Atlanta returned over a month later, the tension returned with them. The clock was to be set with one second left, the score tied, and Atlanta with the ball at their end of the court. Before the clock was started, the Hawks called a time-out to move the ball to midcourt. We had worked on our defense for weeks. We called it our *two months, one second defense*. We had to keep Atlanta from scoring and then try to beat them in overtime.

Tom Boerwinkle deflected the inbounds pass and everyone dove for the ball. Lou Hudson of the Hawks came up with it, dribbled once and then realized that time *had* to have run out. But the buzzer hadn't sounded. In all the preparations for the replay, the clock had been set, but the buzzer hadn't! That made us look terrible. Richie Guerin, the Hawks player-coach, really got into it. "See, the buzzer doesn't work!" he screamed. "They've had weeks to work on it and it still doesn't work!"

We wound up losing the game by six in overtime. Later, when I looked at the video tape of the last second, I saw the beautiful play which had been devised by Guerin. Joe Caldwell had been wide open. If the pass had been complete, he'd have had an easy lay up. (I liked the play and used it later against Atlanta to beat them in the last two seconds on their court. "That play looks familiar," Guerin said.)

Besides gaining new fans from the hassle, we also got a new scoreboard clock at the Stadium.

Jerry Krause was still around, so I remained unhappy with our scouting situation. I took it upon myself to try to see as many college ballgames as I could when we had nights off. Just traveling and coaching during a regular season is enough to run me ragged, but I felt we needed an edge when the player draft came around. I saw about 35 college games during the 1969-70 season.

I flew down to scout a game in Charlotte, N.C., one night, planning to fly directly to Boston for our game the next evening. Besides being exhausted, I was fighting a cold. After the game in Charlotte I took a couple of college coaches out for a late dinner and didn't get to bed until about 2 A.M.

My flight to Boston left Charlotte at 6 A.M., and I didn't get much more sleep on the plane. We stopped in Washington, D.C., because of mechanical problems and were laid over there for about four hours. I couldn't sleep because I had to be ready to run when the plane was ready. I felt miserable and my head throbbed.

My watch read 3:15 when I finally got to my hotel in Boston. I was dead. I asked the desk clerk to give me a wakeup call at 6:30 so I could get to the Boston

Garden early enough for a television interview. There
was nothing wrong with my alarm clock, but I wasn't
about to trust my hearing it in my condition.

When I opened the door to my room I heard a
low squeal. In the dimness I made out a young woman
sitting next to a sleeping baby. "There must be a
mixup," I said, backing out. "I'm sorry."

I was in no mood for confusion. "There's somebody
in the damn room," I snapped at the desk clerk. He
apologized and tried to make up for it.

"I'll give you a nice big suite," he said. I didn't care
if it was a cot in a single room, but the suite was a
mess. And so was I. A couple of dozen champagne
bottles and corks were strewn all over the floor. That
wouldn't have bothered me, but the beds were di-
sheveled too. I stomped back down to the desk.

I was mad. "You got a clean, empty room in this
place?" I said. I could hardly see straight. The clerk
was very apologetic and gave me the key to my third
room. I didn't thank him. I just went straight up.

I was half asleep as I stripped to my shorts and put
my watch and alarm clock on the bureau. I set the
alarm for 6:15 and flopped onto the bed, asleep. At
6:30 the night shift desk clerk checked his list and
made a wakeup call to my original room. At 7:30
Bull trainer Jerry McCann called the house detective
to check the room I had originally checked in.

At 8 o'clock I woke up and looked at my alarm
clock. It read 10 after 6. *Good*, I thought, *five more
minutes to sleep.* I slept for just another couple of
minutes and opened my eyes, not moving. I sensed
the blackness outside. Something wasn't right.

I bolted to a sitting position and grabbed my
watch. It still read 3:15, and I had set the alarm by

it! I felt cold all through. *The game!* I had to find out what time it was. I called the hotel operator and let it ring four times, grabbing my shirt and pants with my free hand. No answer. I called the long distance operator.

"Long distance, your call pl—"

"Are you in Boston?" I asked.

"Yes, sir. Your call p—"

"What time is it here?"

"Thirteen after eight, sir."

I hung up and jammed myself into my shirt and pants. Grabbing my sport coat and raincoat, I scurried down the hall buckling, zipping, and buttoning as I dragged a comb through my hair. In the elevator I barely got myself presentable before sprinting across the lobby to a taxi.

"Get me to the Garden as fast as you can. I'm really in a hurry. I'll double whatever's on the meter."

"What's happenin'?" the cabbie asked.

"My team's playing over there," I said. "Let's go!"

"Who's that?" he asked as he took off, "the Chicago Bulls?"

"Yeah."

"What're you, the center? Ha ha ha!"

"No, I'm the coach." By now he was doing almost 80 miles an hour. Driving the limit, he'd have gotten me to the stadium in 25 minutes. He made it in less than half the time, but it seemed like an hour to me. My fatigue was forgotten. I had a bad feeling of dread. We had lost two straight, and here I was late to a game.

"The game started at eight," the cabbie said.

"Don't shit me," I said. "I know that!"

At the Garden I threw him a bill for about three

times the price on the meter. "Is that enough?" I called over my shoulder as I dashed into the Garden.

"Hey, Buddy," he shouted, "call me the *next* time you're late!"

A guard at the gate recognized me. His mouth dropped open.

"I know," I said, tossing him my raincoat. "Hang this up for me, will ya?"

I got to courtside just as a timeout had been called. The players were huddled around the bench. Suddenly I appeared among them. "Where've you been?" Boerwinkle gasped.

I was too shook to think of a lie. "I slept in."

"Damn!" Boerwinkle said.

The Bulls had been playing great up to then. Somehow I couldn't shake the feeling that I was an outsider. I couldn't get involved. Their game suffered and midway through the third quarter the Celtics caught up. By early in the fourth quarter Boston was up by six and I was furious. I shouted a couple of things at the ref and was immediately hit with two technicals and ejected. I had come late, and now I was leaving early. The next day a Boston sports page headline read, "He Shoulda Stood in Bed."

In the dressing room after the game, Chet Walker said in his characteristic, dry way, "Coach, what would it have cost me if I had been late?"

"Five hundred," I said.

"You gonna pay anything?" he asked.

"I'll pay a hundred," I said.

"How come not five hundred?"

"'Cause I'm worth one-fifth of what you guys are."

I haven't yet shaken the feeling of dread I had when I realized I had overslept. Even now I'll often wake up with a start in the middle of the night, wondering if I've done it again. I dream about it and hate the thought of it almost as much as the thought of losing.

Late during the second season we had a tight game against the Lakers at Los Angeles. We led by two with about 10 seconds to play, and Clem Haskins was at the foul line. If he just makes one we ice the victory. He missed the first, then looked to our bench before shooting the second. He made it and the Lakers didn't have time to score. As we ran to the locker room Jerry McCann said, "Coach, you've got problems on the team. The bench is cheering against you!"

"Whad'ya mean?"

"They yelled *pressure* when Clem was shooting the free throws. They wanted him to miss. They wanted us to lose!"

I had been thrilled with the win, but now I was mad. I burst into the dressing room, screaming.

"Who yelled *pressure?* Who did it?" Bob Kaufman raised one finger sheepishly and pointed to himself and Lloyd Peterson. I went on a 10-minute tirade about team attitude, wanting your friends to win instead of hoping your coach will lose just because you aren't playing as much as you think you should. It would have been easy for Kaufman and Peterson to interrupt my spiel and explain that they were trying to encourage Clem and had no thought of wanting us to lose, but they couldn't. I found out later that Elgin Baylor had sent a bucket of chicken to the dressing room, and the substitutes from the end of the bench had gotten to it first. They stuffed the best pieces into their mouths and had just begun to chew when I started in on them. They held their full mouths shut during the whole harangue. There I was, spouting off while they were choking on chicken!

Sloan pulled a groin muscle and missed 29 games during 1969-70. When he came back I kept him as my combination third guard and third forward. We were in a dog fight with San Francisco and Phoenix for the last playoff spot in our division, and I could taste it. We all could. Our last seven games in the regular season were scheduled on consecutive nights in different cities, so we were worn to a frazzle. Our third game was against the Milwaukee Bucks in Madison, Wisc. Sloan was injured again. He pulled three ribs away from his sternum and broke another rib in his back in a collision with Bob Dandridge. We didn't publicize it for fear that if he was able to play, someone might take advantage of him and try to get him out of the game.

We were to bus to O'Hare after the game and fly to Omaha to play Cincinnati. McCann advised that Sloan just stay in Chicago when we stopped over. Sloan disagreed. "I've just got to go with you," he said. We arranged for the team doctor to meet us at O'Hare. He checked Jerry over and said it was Sloan's decision. Jerry went with us.

He didn't sleep at all in Omaha, but sat up all night in pain. In the morning McCann said he still thought Sloan should be sent home. I agreed.

We had to take our packed bags to the stadium in Omaha because we were to fly back to Chicago for a game the next evening. I went to the stadium early and was feeling down. It was a bad day, Jerry was hurt, and the season was coming to an end.

As I trudged into the dressing room in Omaha, who

should be there but Sloan. "I thought you'd gone home," I said.

"Well, I was walking the streets," he said. "And I saw this elastic band in a store window and thought it might work for me. I feel all right with it on and I think I'd like to play."

He looked like he needed some sleep. "Hey, Jer, I don't know," I said.

"Well, just let me warm up and see."

The elastic band he had bought looked like a small girdle. He still couldn't lift his arms above his shoulders, and Chet Walker, Jerry McCann, and I had to help him put his uniform on. "This is foolish," I said. "You know you don't have to go through this."

"Well, let me warm up at least." I've always had a policy that I won't dictate to a player about injuries. If he says he's sick or hurt, I'll believe him. But if he says he's okay, I can't disagree. Only he knows whether or not the pain is such that he can't play. If he shows up on the bench with his uniform on, I'll play him as if he's 100 per cent healthy. Sloan looked terrible. He walked in a half crouch and hobbled to the court.

Usually I stay in the dressing room while the players are warming up. This time I wanted a look at Jerry. I had to know if he'd be any kind of a backup for the starting five. I had settled on Weiss and Haskins at guards, Walker and Love at forwards, and Boerwinkle at center. Jerry appeared to be in considerable pain as he tried to shoot, but midway through the warm up he jogged over to me.

"Coach," he said, "you know I'd never try to tell you how to do anything, and I don't want to offend you, but can I say something?"

"Sure."

"Well, if I were you, I'd start me while I'm warm."
All I could do was measure his maturity and my
respect for him. Only he could measure the pain.
I said okay. If he wanted to play, I figured he was
better off playing. (Of course, if a doctor said not to
play an injured player, I'd keep him out, regardless
of what the player said.)

Jerry played well that night, scoring about a dozen
and containing Oscar Robertson as well as could be
expected for a man in his condition. The pain was
getting to him, though. That became obvious when I
called a timeout. We were trailing 53-50.

"Look," I said, "they're not that intense. They're
already out of the playoffs. We have everything to
gain. Let's stay close and don't let them get too far
ahead." We were dog tired playing our fifth game in
five nights.

As the huddle broke up, Sloan said, "C'mon guys,
don't give up now! We've made up 30 points in a
quarter before, we can do it again!" The other players
and I did a double take at Sloan and the scoreboard.
I called Jerry back as the others took the court.

"How many points are we down, Jerry?" I asked,
smiling.

"We're down thirty, Coach," he said. "But we'll
get 'em."

"What's the score?" I asked him, no longer smiling.
"83-50."

"Look again, Jerry. It's 53-50!"

"Oh."

It wasn't like Sloan to lose track of 30 points, but
he had.

We went on to win the game in overtime, largely due to two clutch plays, one a steal, by Bob Weiss. He grabbed the ball and raced the length of the court, slowing up a bit so he could score just before the buzzer and keep the Royals from getting the ball again. Our playoff spot was cinched. We didn't know if we'd finish third and play the first place Atlanta Hawks, or finish fourth and play second place Los Angeles. At that point, we didn't care. We had made the playoffs.

We were interviewed on Chicago television after the game and everyone got a chance to say a little something. Jerry Sloan said, "This reminds me of college ball. It's really a privilege to be in Chicago." That made me feel good, and so did something I heard at a restaurant afterward. We had a couple of hours to kill before our return flight, so we went out to eat as a team. We ran into Jack Madden, an NBA ref.

"You guys did a helluva job this year," he said. We weren't even a .500 ballclub, but we had drawn 10,000 fans per game and had made the playoffs. My relationship with most NBA officials had long since begun to deteriorate. I had never talked to one informally before. It seemed to me that the Big Sky Conference out west had more consistent refereeing, and when the calls continually seemed to go against us, I began to take it personally. It wasn't so much that I thought the refs were down on me, but down on the Bulls.

We were a second division team. We didn't have any nationally acclaimed superstars. It was easier to call fouls and violations on us than on the winners. I began to speak my mind, and it cost me. I had been fined heavily for saying, "Fifth place teams get fifth rate officials," so it was an unusual experience to chat informally with Madden.

I've mellowed a bit on the treatment of superstars. I still don't think it's right to totally ignore an obvious call, but many of the established stars have been in this league for several years. They've paid their dues and they deserve some respect, even the benefit of the doubt once in a while from a ref. I didn't feel that way at all during my second season, though. And I was beginning to develop a reputation. A reputation I didn't enjoy, and which I've never lived down.

At the end of the regular season we had won 39 games. I told my wife, "If a guy could have a season without serious injuries and coach a .500 team, this wouldn't be a bad job at all." We had to flip a coin with Phoenix to see who would get credit for third place, since our records were identical. I guess we won it. We didn't get any more money, and we wound up "winning" the right to play Atlanta instead of the ailing Lakers (Chamberlain had undergone knee surgery).

The Hawks had little trouble with us in the first round of the playoffs. We only won one and they blew us out in five games. We lost the first two badly in Atlanta, then lost a close one at home, so it was just a matter of time after that. We were thrilled to have made it, and the fans seemed to enjoy the excitement of playoff basketball. I was beginning to get the feel of coaching in the NBA, and while I wasn't married to the city of Chicago, I was happier than before and ready to stay in the league.

I hoped that 1970-71 would be even better for me and for the Bulls, but I had no inkling just how good it would be. I knew that a 50-win season was an NBA measuring stick, but I wasn't ready to even hope for that yet. I should have. It was just around the corner.

CHAPTER **8**

C R O W N E D

PAT WILLIAMS had renegotiated some contracts during his first few months on the scene, so some of the underpaid ballplayers were getting a better shake. Player morale was up. "Maybe I ought to hit you for a raise too," I said, only half serious.

"Come on in," he said. And he *was* serious. He tore up my contract, which had one more year to run at $22,500, and wrote me a three-year deal for $25,000, $27,500, and $30,000. The money didn't make that much difference to me, but the vote of confidence was encouraging. Going into the 1970-71 season, I was at $27,500 and ready to give the NBA a chance to keep me from dreaming about coaching at a major university.

We lost Walt Wesley in the expansion draft that season, so I was without an adequate backup center. I knew I'd have to give up a starter to get a decent center, but it was difficult to see who might be expendable. Pat and I looked to the college player draft for a guard who would be able to replace Clem Haskins. We thought we'd found one in Jimmy Collins. We drafted him and paid him big money, trading Haskins to Phoenix for Jim Fox, a backup center.

We had lost Bob Kaufman to Philadelphia as a second part of the Washington for Walker trade. It was just as well for us and for Bob. Philadelphia turned around and traded him to Buffalo, so he wound up with an expansion team. They used him as their starting center and he made the all-star team. Now he's a qualified forward in the NBA and I'm sure it's due to the valuable confidence-building experience he got in Buffalo which he wouldn't have received in Chicago. He simply wouldn't have been able to crack our lineup for the playing time needed for his development.

It didn't take us long to realize that we had made a mistake in counting so heavily on the rookie Collins and not covering ourselves properly for the loss of Haskins. With Fox on the bench I was satisfied with the centers, but when Collins didn't perform at guard as I had hoped, I had to start Bob Weiss. Weiss was more than capable of starting, but I've always felt he was more valuable to me as my third guard. With his deft outside shooting and his ability to make the big steal, he was the ideal man to have ready for an early substitution. But now he was starting along with Sloan, Walker, Love, and Boerwinkle.

We were competing and playing better, but I was

disappointed that the bench wasn't as strong as it could be. I wanted to free up Weiss to be third guard again, and when we played Philadelphia early in the season, I saw a possible solution.

Matt Goukas had held out on the 76ers in a contract dispute. When he was put into the lineup against us, the Philadelphia fans booed him. I liked his style of play. He was a crisp passer and a playmaker. He wasn't a big scorer, but was rather a perimeter player, a precise, team man. I told Pat I thought the 76ers might be willing to trade Matt, at least I was sure he'd be ready to leave a town where the fans didn't appreciate him. I was right. Philadelphia let him go for a second round draft choice, a real steal. With Mattie in our lineup, the pieces seemed to fall in place. Weiss was fresh and ready when I needed him and became as good a third guard as there is in the NBA. He's also a super intelligent ballplayer, the type I like to take with me to coaching clinics.

The Bulls were starting to compete fairly evenly, even with the league leaders. We seldom got blown out of a game, and playing Chicago was no longer a breather for the NBA big boys. After staying close to opponents the first time around and making them earn their victories, we gained confidence and realized that if we could hang in the next time we faced them, we could knock them off. We started sticking up for ourselves and working hard. For the first time since I had come to Chicago, the Bulls were playing better than .500 ball consistently. We had some fun that season too.

I have a team meeting about half an hour before each game where we informally talk over the assignments and strategy. Then we have a moment of

silent prayer. I ask all the players to respect that
moment of silence, because whether or not they believe in anything, there are those of us who do. I
pray that the players will play to their potential, that
the fans will be entertained, that there won't be any
serious injuries, and that the team that should win
will win. But, quite honestly, my silent prayer is not
always that detailed. In fact, more than half the time
I just daydream. I'm quite a daydreamer anyway, but
when you've had a silent prayer 50 times already
during the season, it can become more of a ritual
than a meaningful moment. Well, we were about to
play Phoenix, and I had asked the players to have a
moment of silence. I bowed my head and held my
hands behind my back. I began to sway ever so
slightly as most people do when their eyes are closed.
As I leaned forward I brushed against a greasy mass
of analgesic balm on the side of the trash barrel in
the middle of the room. "Damn it to hell," I said
quietly in the middle of my reverent prayer.

The startled players tried not to crack up. Bob
Biel, who had joined the team as trainer after a two-
year absence, tried to wash out the balm in the sink
with hot water and soap, but it was no use. Now I
had a pair of slacks with grease *and* water all over
the lap. (I didn't stand much during the game. And
when I did I kept my hands folded in front of me like
a little boy who had wet his pants!)

Another time during the silent prayer I got daydreaming and almost forgot to end it with my usual,
"Let's go!" The silence usually lasts just 30 seconds or
so, but I guess I half dozed off and kept the players
there more than two full minutes. There I was, head
bowed in reverence with the players peeking at each

other and wondering if they should tap me on the
shoulder. They were about to when I came around.
"Let's go!" I said.

Up until about two weeks before the end of the
season, I still held out faint hopes for a possible
university coaching job. But then we made our final
push. Things had gelled, and we quickly neared the
50-win mark. The trademark of an established contender. I could hardly believe it. It was like running
a four-minute mile. We finished fast, winding up with
51 victories and more momentum than any other
team in the NBA. We even got national publicity calling us the hottest team. I thought we were ready to
really make some noise.

For the second time in my three years, and the
fourth time in the Bulls' five-year history, Chicago
had made the playoffs. We didn't want history to
repeat itself. The Bulls had never won a road playoff
game, and they had never gotten past the first round.
Unfortunately, we were matched up against the
Lakers. You guessed it, we kept the string alive. We
lost every game in Los Angeles, but made it interesting
by winning every game in Chicago. It was terribly
frustrating to think that with the home court advantage we might have won an eighth game (and the
playoff could have gone on forever).

I was kicked out of one of the Chicago victories.
We were losing in the first half and we had been getting some bad calls. I started hassling the refs, and
with the second technical I was sent to the dressing
room. That didn't bother me much, because I thought
it would psyche up the players. I got tired of listening
to the game on the radio, so I thought I'd try to sneak
into the stands. After all, it *was* a playoff game.

And the Bulls were surging back. I didn't want to miss it, despite an automatic $500 fine for leaving the dressing room after being ejected.

I was caught. Whoever represented the league office was very thorough. He even had my seat number recorded. I don't suppose it helped much that I was sending messages back and forth to the bench. On top of the automatic fine, I was nailed with $1,000 more. (Really, the league has always been very lenient with me. Even when I get fined heavily I can look back to times when I should have been fined and wasn't.)

Many fans think it's an act when a coach gets a little carried away. Or they think he thinks it's cute. Actually, I'm usually ashamed of myself afterwards. It's just that I get so wrapped up, so involved in what's happening that the game becomes an emotional conflict. It's no longer my job, my business, my trade, It's more like my family. The men on the floor are my kids and I care about them, I want to protect them, I want some control over what happens to them. I'll see myself on film after a game and I can hardly believe some of my actions.

And I'm not personally down on any of the refs. I think some are unqualified, but I have no animosity toward them. I'd kinda like to get to know a few of them a little better. But I probably never will. They live very lonely lives. During my first three seasons I got so tired of fighting Klein and the refs and the league that I continued to wonder if I wouldn't be better off back coaching a college team. In college a coach has more latitude with the refs. When I first got into the NBA I heard Richie Guerin of Atlanta screaming at the refs (Richie was taught to whisper in a saw mill), and I assumed that was what the coaches could get away with. Wrong. At least not this coach.

So what if I yell at the refs? I yell at my players. And I yell at myself. I'm that type of a guy. I push myself and my team hard and I expect an official to be as up for the game as we are.

I'm more compassionate toward the refs since I first realized that *all* of their games are road games. I talked to one of the refs on a plane once and he mentioned that he had worked a game two nights before in San Francisco, the night before in Seattle, and he had a game in Cleveland coming up. Three games in three nights, almost coast to coast. There was no way he could get up for that third game. It wasn't an important game for him. It couldn't be.

We have some officials in the NBA who don't belong here, but it takes a hell of a man to be a ref. The staff that was designed for a league of 10 teams has not been beefed up despite the addition of expansion teams. Several of the good refs jumped to the American Basketball Association and a short staff was left shorter.

There's no way a ref can win. The winning coach will forget a dozen bad calls, but the loser will remember the one that "turned our game around, broke our backs." I know I do. A ref goes into a game knowing that he can't work it perfectly. His talent does not compare with the task he is expected to do. There is too much to see in too short a time. And the calls are so subjective. The players are geniuses. They know all the officials and they know all the tricks. They know when the official is watching them, and they know when he isn't.

I respect the good officials, and I don't get into too much trouble with them. I think most of the trouble I get into is with the young refs over drastic mistakes.

At my own basketball camp for boys I've spent a little time in the ref's shoes. It's an enlightening experience. Once I was working a game between junior high campers coached by Gene Visscher and Phil Johnson. I called a foul against one of Phil's players. "What the hell?" Phil shouted.

Why, you son of a bitch, was my first thought. And the next three times down the court I looked for things to call on his team. Refs are human. They react to situations like that. As we start each ball game, we are supposed to be innocent. The slate has been wiped clean. But no one can tell me that the ref has cleared from his mind the last time I tried to make him feel like a fool for missing a call. Half of my technicals are due to my reputation, I think. Knowing that the refs don't forget the treatment I give them should teach me something, I guess. But I get involved in a game and see an obvious bad call, and I have to speak up.

During that first 50-win season I had my first game in which I was hit with three technicals. Two means an automatic ejection, so I guess it's some kind of a record. They can call a technical for anything they want. I've been called for rising four inches off the bench, without saying a word. Of course, they have to have total control on the floor. That's the only way the thing would work, so that's the way we want it. But sometimes a technical is not the result of what has actually happened during the game. It could be the culmination of a two-week feud, during which you've hassled a ref in three or four different games.

Finally, he's had enough and the first time you open your mouth, boom. Sometimes they've had enough of you before you start, and other times they're more patient and understanding. I've had refs see me throw a towel all the way across the court and ignore it. Then I'll stand and glare at them with my hands on my hips and they nail me with a T.

There's one ref in the league who gets fatter as the season goes on. That's almost impossible, but somehow he does it. And he doesn't like to hear me remind him of it. When he misses a call I'll often say, "That's why you're the only damn guy in the league who gains weight during the season. You're not hustling. You're not running!" Boom, the T.

Once I hassled a ref and told him some uncomplimentary things and he kicked me out on the first technical. A few weeks later he blew some calls in Atlanta, and Hawks' coach Cotton Fitzsimmons called him over. "Whatever Motta said about you, I double it!" He said. Fitzsimmons listened to the rest of the game from the locker room.

I'm not particularly proud of the game in which I got three technicals before being removed, but it *was* interesting. Lenny Wilkens, one of my favorites and a guy who plays guard the way it should be played, got away with a violation right in front of our bench. I protested the call and was hit with a technical. The ref who hit me with it was not even the ref I'd been talking to, so that upset me. "Protecting your junior partner?" I taunted. "Can't he take care of himself?" That cost me number two and I was thumbed out. But it had happened too quickly. I wasn't ready to leave. I walked out to the foul line where Wilkens was about to shoot the free throw.

"Get him out of here," Wilkens told the ref. "Lemme shoot the technical."

"Get out," the ref said. I didn't move. Wilkens was disgusted and didn't see any point in standing there with the ball as long as I was in front of him, so he flipped the ball to me and walked away. I put the ball under my arm and went to give Bob Biel some instructions for the game before heading for the locker room.

"Give me the ball or I'll give you another technical," the ref said.

"Why not?" I said. "You've already given me two."

He said okay and hit me with another. I was furious. He reached for the ball. I spit on it and tossed it to him. "You s.o.b.," he said.

"I wish I'd have shit on it," I said. I had made a fool of myself, and he took care of me. I was fined $1,000, and I'm surprised (and lucky) I wasn't suspended.

The strangest antic I ever got away with in a game happened in Detroit. We were down by two near the end of the game when Detroit's Otto Moore swept one of our shots right out of the basket. A foul was called, but I jumped up raising both fists in the air and shouting, "Goal tending! Goal tending!" I was ignored, but the ball bounced right into my hands. I was so incensed that the call had been missed that I felt like kicking the ball. The refs were busy pulling the bodies apart after the collision at the hoop, so I thought, *Why not?*

I dropped that ball and drove my toe into it. The thrust of my beautiful punt lifted me right off the ground in a follow through that would have thrilled George Halas. The ball soared a good 30 yards into the second balcony of Cobo Hall. It dropped right into the hands of a big black man who must have weighed close to 300 pounds. I knew before the ball got to him that I had made a terrible mistake. I backed onto the bench and sat on my hands, looking the other way. Jim Fox said, "Coach, I didn't see you do that. Tell me I didn't see you do that."

"Do what?" I said.

The refs had the teams organized again and the guys lined up for a foul shot. Referee Don Murphy asked, "Where's the ball?" The Detroit players were pointing into the balcony and over at me. I looked as innocent as I could, and since neither ref had seen the kick, they just got another ball. With that, Butch van Breda Kolff, the Detroit coach, raced onto the floor and was rapped with a T. The place went up for grabs.

The kick had been caught perfectly on Chicago television, so there was no denying it. I didn't know what to say to the reporters after the game. I mean, how do you explain that you've flat blown your cool?

"Why'd you kick the ball?" was the first question.

I tried to appear as bananas as they thought I was

"I *had* to," I said, straight-faced.

"What do you mean, you *had* to?"

"I just did. I had to."

"But *why*?"

"Well, that ball was full of bad air."

The sportswriters looked at each other knowingly, and at me sympathetically, and slowly backed away. No more questions.

(The man who caught the ball reluctantly gave it up to the ushers. The next time we were in Detroit I took him an autographed ball, but I couldn't find him.)

I guess the story never got back to the commissioner or I'd have been suspended, or at least fined. The Knicks had played Detroit the day after the incident, so the next time we played New York, their star forward, Dave DeBusschere, told me what van Breda Kolff's reaction had been.

"He said he was mad because he wanted to be the first coach in the league to get three technicals in one game," big Dave laughed. "He's devising a plan now where he can get four."

"Four?" I said. "How's he gonna do that?"

"Well, he says he'll get two early in the first half and get kicked out. Then, because the refs have such bad memories, he'll come back out with the team after intermission and get two more in the second half!"

Later that year one of my friends sent me a certificate for winning the Golden Toe Award as the Lou Groza of basketball. van Breda Kolff wrote and challenged me to a punting contest. No way. He'd been an All-American soccer player in college.

Somehow, in spite of my increasing reputation as a trouble maker and my crazy run ins with the officials, the league sportswriters voted me the NBA Coach of the Year. I wasn't too excited about it because it was announced after the last game of the playoffs with the Lakers. It was nice to receive the plaque from commissioner Walter Kennedy on nationwide television, but I was disappointed over being eliminated from the playoffs in what I thought was to be the Bulls' year.

Anyway, the Coach of the Year award is kind of a rotated thing. I've coached better since and haven't won it. And the coaches of the championship contenders seldom get it either. I guess it's good for the writers to pass it around and let the new coaches enjoy the flattery and the encouragement, but I don't think as much of the award as say the all-defensive team which is chosen by the NBA coaches. I shared the thrill equally with Jerry Sloan and Norm Van Lier this past season when they were named the all-pro defensive guards. It was a tribute to them and to the Bulls. And it helps refute the charges by the press and other "experts" that Sloan and Van Lier are anything other than aggressive professionals.

At the end of the 1970-71 season a friend of mine asked if I would call the Dallas Chaparrels' and recommend him to the general manager as a good candidate for the coaching job down there. I didn't know how aware an American Basketball Association executive would be of an NBA coach, but I called anyway.

Bob Briner, the Dallas G.M., sounded like a nice guy. We talked awhile about my friend, and I told Bob I was sure he could handle the job. Just before I hung up I casually asked, "What kind of money are you talking about?"

"Oh, we're probably in the neighborhood of $30,000 a year or so."

"Hell," I said, "that's more than I'm making."

"You're kidding."

"Nope."

"You've been in the NBA what, three years? And you're Coach of the Year this year and that's all you're making?"

"That's right."

"Well, why don't you come down and work here?"

I thought he was kidding. "You don't have enough money," I said, chuckling.

"Try us," he said.

"You're not serious."

"I am. Give me a try."

A few things raced through my mind. The ABA had lost some big name players to the NBA. Getting the Coach of the Year to jump might help start reversing the trend. I wasn't sure I was any more qualified than the guy I had recommended, but I figured, why not see if he's really serious?

"Oh, let's see," I said lightly, "I'd want $50,000 a year for three years to move."

"That's in the ballpark," Briner said. "We can talk about that. Are you serious?"

"If you're talking that kind of money, I've gotta listen to you." He said he'd meet me in Chicago in a few days.

I told Pat Williams about the call and told him that I'd probably be leaving to take the offer. I assured him that Dallas was in no way guilty of tampering with a coach under contract. "I initiated the contact," I said.

"Well, if you've gotta go, you've gotta go," Pat said.

I called the friend who had asked me to recommend *him* and explained what had happened. He understood and was very gracious, though I'm sure he regretted choosing me to recommend him.

Janice and I met with Briner at the O'Hare Inn the following Monday. I knew immediately that I was dealing with a straightforward, sincere guy. He was understanding, and was ready to bend at every point to accommodate me. Since I liked my team and my work in Chicago, in spite of my hassles with the owners, I decided that the Dallas job would have to be perfect in every respect for me to accept it.

I asked for the right to choose my own assistant and scout. I wanted to be in charge of drafting, negotiating, signing, and trades. And I wanted Dallas to take over the payments on a life insurance policy I had purchased. Briner agreed to it all, even my choice of Phil Johnson as assistant and scout. He invited Janice and me and Phil and his wife to visit Dallas. Now I was really excited.

Phil had lost a total of 15 games in three years as head coach at Weber State. The first year I was gone he had coached probably Weber's best team ever. His teams had made the university division NCAA playoffs three years in a row, so outside of a national championship, Phil had done about all he could at Weber. And Gene Visscher was there to keep our system going. Phil was ready to try his hand at pro coaching.

The night before I was to meet Phil in Dallas, Pat came to the house. "Let me tell what the Bulls have to offer," he said.

"I'm not using this as a wedge," I said. "I'm not interested in a counter offer."

"We were going to offer you a raise, anyway," he said. "We got together and set up a nice deal. There is no intention of trying to sway you one way or the other. It's just one offer so you'll know what you can have if you stay. We're not in a position to start bidding with another club. This is our only offer. You decide."

The offer was about the same as I had received from Dallas, including picking up the payment of my life insurance policy, some deferred payments, fringe benefits, and a car. But this was for five years. The life insurance deal was important to me, and I didn't need any more money. There are already enough people around who think, and publish, that I make twice as much as I do, so I don't need the headaches of more money.

I had bought the life insurance plan when I got into the NBA because I had given up retirement benefits by leaving Weber State. Up until recently there was no pension plan in the NBA. Even now the plan is inadequate for the responsibility.

When I came to the NBA I couldn't understand the philosophy of the league. I guess they thought the main duties of a coach were to sit at one end of the bench, pick the players who start, get them to the game on time, and wear a tie and coat. Things have improved, but the way coaches are paid and treated has made me wonder if I wasn't just a glorified cheerleader.

The players have big salaries and pension plans. And I don't begrudge them that. Players win games, and people don't come to watch coaches coach. They come to watch players play. No one stays in the league much longer than 10 years, so you have to get what you can while you can. The same is true of coaches. Football owners are realizing this and are paying their coaches well and setting up security programs for them so they can confidently get their systems working. Baseball owners are worse than basketball, with half the managers getting fired before they can build decent programs. Walter Alston of the Dodgers is the only manager I can think of who has been around long enough for his teams to take on some of his flavor and personality.

The good owners in the NBA are catching on and

realizing that the coaches should be taken care of. It's encouraging, at least.

Well, it was good to know that the Bulls were interested in keeping me around if they could. The offer didn't turn my head though, not consciously anyway. I went to Dallas thinking that I would probably take the Chaparral job. After seeing the facilities and talking with the owners, I was sure I would take it. And it was obvious that Phil wanted to go too.

When I returned to Chicago, the Bulls' radio announcer, Jack Fleming, was at the airport to greet me. We had become friends. "I think I'm going to Dallas," I told him.

"I don't think you should," he said. We talked for hours. Basically he just tried to remind me of all the benefits of staying in a big city, an NBA city, where I had experience. Phil and his wife really wanted to go to Dallas, and Janice was still a rock. It was my decision alone.

Fleming reminded me that Dallas will always be Cowboy football country. The basketball team, especially an ABA club, would not be popular in the football hotbed. The Midwest is basketball country. Pat Williams also said I could bring Phil in as my assistant and scout, but what really turned me around was one of my players.

He came to me and told me that if I left, he would quit basketball. It wasn't a threat. It was a fact. He didn't want to play for anyone else. It really touched me. I didn't change my mind on that basis alone, but it was the one last factor I needed. I decided to stay, and Phil became my assistant. I looked forward to the 1971-72 season with more anticipation than ever. And with good reason. It would be the most productive in Chicago history.

Pat Williams was happy, and despite the fact that he's a nervous, emotional type, he didn't show it much. When there was bad news he'd say, "Not so good." And when news was good he said little. He was very straightforward. He believes that everything is pre-planned by God and will work out for the best one way or the other. "It's God's way."

That summer I went on a USO-sponsored tour of Vietnam with Bob Love and two other ballplayers, Dale Schlueter and McCoy McLemore. We played a lot of exhibition games and shook a lot of hands. Much of the work was in the hospitals, which we didn't relish.

We were flown around Vietnam in a helicopter, and publicity preceded us. There was always quite a crowd. In the northern sector we stopped at a base where one soldier had been particularly anxious to meet us. A few hours before we arrived he had been critically wounded. As he gained consciousness every so often, he asked to get to meet us when we arrived. Only one of us could visit him in intensive care. None of us wanted to. We didn't know what he'd look like or how we'd react to him.

I went in. He looked so young. Tubes ran in and out of him from every direction. His foot had been blown off, and his intestines lay next to him in a plastic bag. I fought not to look shocked, but I couldn't play candy-striper either. "Pretty rough, huh?" I said when he opened his eyes.

He smiled weakly. "You're the coach of the Bulls," he said.

"I hear you were in a tough battle."

He rolled his eyes and didn't speak. I felt pretty lousy. Somehow the war seemed worthless. And, hey, I'm somewhat of a flagwaver. I just didn't see anything in that whole damn country that told me why Americans were over there getting blown to bits. Standing there talking to a kid whose intestines were in a sack, I was overwhelmed with the feeling that we should be out of there. We should be home.

I told the players to go with an open mind, to not embarrass ourselves or the league or the country by forming any opinions. But when I saw the millions and millions of dollars worth of American war machinery over there, I had to wonder why they hadn't come up with a better machine for harvesting rice than a wooden plow pulled by a water buffalo. How are those people ever going to fill all the craters left by the bombs? How long does it take barbed wire to recycle? Do those people want or need what we were trying to give them? One of the people we were over there fighting to protect tried to steal my camera. Another spit on me.

There were a lot of goldbricking American soldiers in the hospitals too. I'd ask one or two kids why they were in the hospital and they'd say, "Oh, I have a bad back," or "I still don't feel well." Shit. In the next bed is a kid who seems happy to talk to anyone. When I ask him what happened, he whips the cover back and shows me the stump, all that remains of his leg.

I found out how naive I was about drugs too. The absolute boredom of Vietnam made it easy for thousands of good, wholesome kids to get addicted to drugs. If someone had told me you could smoke heroin, I'd have laughed. In Vietnam, U.S. soldiers started on heroin by smoking it or sniffing it. That's right.

A doctor proved to us how available the stuff was by sending a sergeant out to buy a barrel (about three dollars worth of heroin in a container about the size of the top joint of your little finger). The sergeant was back in minutes. The doctor spread the powder onto the table and examined it. "About 97 per cent pure," he said. "Cut for sale on the street, this would last an average addict one day and would be worth over $80 in the States." Our society is paying the price for that now. Kids were sent home with $3-a-day habits that would turn them into criminals.

I had been against the protests and the marches and some of the charges which had been leveled against the U.S. for our involvement, but now I could see something to it. I decided that if the war was still going on when my son was of age, I'd back him if he decided he didn't want any part of it. I saw kids in Saigon who were the orphans of soldiers from all over the world. There must have been a million vagrants sleeping in the streets, and the orphanages were full.

Strangely, surprisingly to me, the country was beautiful. The shoreline the China sea, the coral, the clear water, the off-shore islands, and the French resorts all seemed so out of place with the sounds of war in the background. Often we traveled at night. It was like flying through a Fourth of July celebration with tracers shooting all around and bombs exploding here and there. It was exciting, and somehow I wasn't scared. It was all a bit unreal.

At each base we'd visit a bunch of guys, I'd talk for a few minutes, then we'd challenge their five best basketball players to   game against our three pros.

Very few of the games were serious, once the soldiers realized that there was no advantage to outnumbering three ballplayers who can jump and shoot at will. By the end of most of the games the soldiers were grabbing the players around the waist to keep them from scoring. It was funny. And fun. The courts weren't much, usually just a bulldozed flat made of mud. The games couldn't go on too long because the temperature was usually near 100 degrees.

I was surprised at how many of the guys were from the Chicago area and had heard of the Bulls. At one base, I ran into a kid I'd coached at Grace High School in Idaho. He had seen one of the leaflets announcing our arrival and had driven over to see me. He held us up a bit, and we were behind schedule, but that didn't bother me in the least. The commanders were always trying to get us on schedule, but they didn't work us hard enough. And we told them so. We thought the tour could have been planned to give us more to do. We were willing to work. We certainly hadn't traveled that far for a vacation.

The best part of the trip was getting to talk to guys who had been to the front lines. I felt I had been involved in a unique civilian experience. They told us what it was really like to fight and fear the Cong.

All the soldiers wanted to know what was happening back in "the world." And they were knowledgeable about sports. They fired questions at us 100 miles an hour. I'm sure it was a thrill for those kids to talk to Bob Love and find out that he's just an ordinary guy, a bit taller and much more fortunate than they, but still a human being. Bob stutters, but only when he's nervous. When those soldiers were so open and curious, Bob was at ease. He and I climbed a 120-

foot communications tower and were scared half out of our wits, but I know when those soldiers see a Bulls' game, they'll remember that and be able to tell their friends.

We flew home with a bunch of soldiers who were leaving Nam for good. It was a strange takeoff. As they filed onto the plane they didn't say one word. There were no smiles or gestures or even whispers. They sat perfectly still and stared straight ahead. All the way down the runway as the plane picked up speed, it was the same. We were puzzled and looked blankly at each other. As soon as the plane left the ground, the soldiers went nuts. They jumped around and cheered, finally assured that they were really on their way home. They had counted the last 100 days on special calendars which were meant to help fight the boredom. In Nam it's feast or famine. You're either in battle with too much to think about, or in a base with nothing to do.

In spite of the obvious inequities, to a man we came back knowing that we live in a hell of a country. It's great to know that I can say what I think, believe the way I want, and pretty much do as I please. Where else in the world . . . ?

CHAPTER 9

CONTENDERS

I FEEL TO THIS DAY that the biggest mistake, talent-wise, the Bulls ever made was trading Mattie Goukas to Cincinnati for Charlie Paulk before the 1971-72 season. We thought we had researched it. I thought Charlie was the tough, hard-nosed third forward we needed to get us over the hump, to take us from respectability to bona fide championship contention. It wasn't long into the pre-season before I realized we had been wrong. We gave up a good player to get what we thought was a better one, and for a month or two we suffered.

In a strange way though, the trade paved the way for the forming of the Bulls' starting unit which did so well and kept us in the running for the next three seasons. Our trading of Goukas to Cincinnati gave them a big guard and two small ones. What they needed was a big center. In the third round of the college draft we had signed Howard Porter of Villanova and Clifford Ray of Oklahoma. I had been talked out of drafting Nate Archibald in the past, even though I predicted, "If we don't draft him, we'll play against him." I had seen Porter in one game and thought he was one of the three best college forwards I had ever seen. I wouldn't back down, so we got him. Ray proved himself quickly in the pre-season, racing up and down the court, jumping and rebounding and playing like an antelope. I tried to get Jim Fox to relax by telling him that I wasn't planning to trade him, but I could see in his eyes that he knew he had to be third center behind Boerwinkle and Ray. Without Goukas we were short a good guard and long on centers. Cincinnati was short a backup center, and long on playmaking guards.

Cincinnati wanted Boerwinkle, but I couldn't see letting him go. He was our starter and he figured into our plans. There were about four guards in the league we were interested in, but we always found ourselves coming back to Cincinnati. We had played them in a pre-season game and our guards couldn't do much against their press. A few games into the regular season I was desperate. We had to have a guard. Cincinnati wasn't about to let Nate Archibald go, so we offered them Fox for Norm Van Lier.

They hesitated. It sounded good to them, but they knew they'd be giving up a lot in Van Lier. He was a scrapper and a hustler, a ball-handling playmaker and super defenseman. "Let us give our centers one more look to see how they're holding up," the Royals said. That night I caught their game on the radio. They were beaten badly at center, so I knew the trade was inevitable. They called in the morning to agree.

That night we were to play the Bullets at Baltimore. I wanted Van Lier as soon as I could get him. Finally I had a real playmaker. I was anxious to see how he'd fit in. "I don't know what the chances are of your making it to Baltimore tonight," I told Norm over the phone, "but it would be great."

"Hey, I'm half there now," he said. "I'm happy to be with Chicago!"

Since he'd been in training camp with us two years earlier, he was familiar with our offense. Playing with Sloan and Weiss was more to his liking. By the time I got to Baltimore, he was waiting for me in the hotel lobby. We went up to my room and I gave him a short course on the offense. He had defended against us for two years, too, so it wasn't totally new to him.

That night I decided to see how he would do spelling Weiss with three or four minutes left in the first period. Norm went nuts. He had 13 assists, 14 points, and a half dozen steals. We won the game easily, and I could sense the excitement of the whole team. It was as if we had a new toy. I rested Jerry Sloan early in the fourth quarter and we just sat there giggling as Norm raced from one end of the court to the other, hitting the open man, deflecting passes, grabbing rebounds, diving for loose balls, setting up plays, and simply taking over. "This is what we need," Jerry and I said almost in unison. And we were right.

Boerwinkle played steady ball for us, Love and Walker were considered one of the best forward combinations in the league, Sloan played his usual intense game, and Norm was all we had hoped he would be. With a week to go in the season we had already broken the club winning record. Our second straight 50-plus win season was in the bag, we had clinched second place and a playoff spot, attendance in Chicago was at an alltime high, and nothing could stop us. We were pretty sure we'd be going head-to-head with the Los Angeles Lakers in the playoffs. After their record 70-win season (losing an incredibly scant 12 games), we would be the underdogs in that one. And that's just the way we wanted it. We had an image of a scrappy, aggressive, physical, battling team with no big name superstars. Almost any team should have been able to out-finesse us and win, but not many did. Our mental attitude, accepting the challenge to fight against the odds, carried us. Then it happened.

With just three games to go before the playoffs, Tom Boerwinkle went up for a rebound. He got off the ground well but while he was in the air I saw him twitch and flinch. He tumbled to the floor and turned toward me. "I popped something in there, Coach," he said. It didn't look too bad. We rested him until the playoffs which opened in a week at Los Angeles.

At the end of the regular season we had won 57 games and we thought we were ready. Yes, even for the Lakers. The loss of every road playoff game in the past still haunted us, but we knew we had to beat the Lakers once on their own floor, and all three times on our own to advance.

In the first game we started quickly and built a 7-3 lead. Tom appeared less mobile, but we hoped he'd loosen up. The Lakers missed a shot and Tom went for the rebound. The knee popped again. This time it was obvious that he couldn't play. We sent him home. Cliff Ray played center for us, but we didn't have time to adjust. Cliff did as well as a rookie center could do against Wilt Chamberlain and a team that had lost only a dozen games. We used Bob Love as our backup center, moving Sloan down to forward when we rested Cliff. It was ridiculous. There was no way we were going to beat Los Angeles without a superhuman effort from our *regular* team. With a makeshift lineup, the games were academic.

We battled the Lakers and made them earn their victories, but they took us in four straight. Los Angeles was so hungry. They had been to the championship seven times in 10 years and had never won. We had not embarrassed ourselves, but after such a super season it was terribly disappointing to see it end so quickly. Once again Chicago had made the playoffs. And once again we had lost our road games (not to mention both home games, too). Once again all we could say was "Wait 'til next year." The fans and writers were disappointed. Two straight second place finishes. Two straight playoff eliminations at the hands of Los Angeles. But we really were excited about 1972-73. We couldn't wait to see what we could do with a healthy Boerwinkle and a team which had, for the most part, been together for three years.

The 1971-72 season remains one of the bright spots of my career. I never once walked into the dressing room worried about dissension, morale, or any kind of a problem. We had one of those rare cooperative team spirits that comes only a few times in a lifetime. Since I had left the high school coaching ranks, that was my most fun year.

During the summer I never knew from one week to the next whether I was going to have a job with the Bulls, or if the team would still be in Chicago, or what. Vacationing in Utah I read and heard rumors daily on the possible sale of the Bulls to various interested money men and groups. In a way I was proud that the owners felt that they could now sell the thriving franchise for a nice profit. For several years it had been nothing but a tax write-off, and for all but a couple of them I'm sure it was a bit of a nuisance. Somehow I got the feeling that they weren't really that thrilled to be owners of the Bulls. In one way that was good because I never had to worry about their trying to tell me how to do my job.

Even Dick Klein kept out of the dressing room and never tried to dictate anything on the playing end. Not who to play or how to play, and for that I was grateful. I'm convinced that he had a sincere dream for the Bulls, and I think he was hoping to hold on until the big television money would come in and salvage the league.

Pat Williams, of course, had a lot to do with turning the franchise around. With Chicagoans interested and the team playing better, the owners found the franchise, which couldn't be given away for a little over a half million dollars a few years before, was now worth millions. It was gratifying, and I guess it was okay that they stood to make quite a profit, but it was strange not knowing what the future held.

Finally the news broke. A new conglomerate in Chicago consisting of people like Lester Crown and Arthur Wirtz bought the club and decided to keep it intact. The only changes had been at the top. The front office would remain the same, the coach and his assistant would stay. The players would not be affected. I was happy. I hoped that the new owners would be basketball fans, at least sportsminded.

Just before I left Utah to head back for training

camp, I received a check and a memo from the previous owners. It was a copied memo which I'm sure went to each person on the staff with varying amounts of money. My check was for four thousand dollars, I guess representing my four years. I was disgusted. It was like going to a big wedding and giving the bride and groom a gift of three dollars. Maybe I wasn't the most important cog in the wheel, but I had stood up for my rights and had coached the team my way. I felt I had had something to do with making the team profitable. And what profit! The owners made so much on the sale that the four thousand dollars was an insult.

I seriously considered ripping the check into little pieces and mailing it back with their memo which read, quaintly, "From all of us to all of you." I talked myself out of destroying it. It would have been expensive revenge, but somehow I still wish I'd done it.

At training camp I was surprised to find that Bob Love hadn't shown up early. It had been his custom to come to camp a few days early. He was always a hard worker. I didn't know much about his contract, but I had understood that he had signed a four-year deal for pretty good money two years before. I didn't figure he would be holding out. And he didn't. At the last minute, just before the first workout with the veterans, he showed up. He didn't try to explain why he hadn't come early as usual, and I didn't ask.

Bob isn't the type to dog it in practice, but that old spark, the enthusiasm, just wasn't there. I was puzzled.

At the end of training camp we were to play several games in Hawaii as a reward for our previous season. Bob Love gave his plane tickets back to Bob Biel and said, "I'm not going." There was little I could do. My realm was limited to the playing end of the game. I reported the incident to Pat Williams. He said he would straighten it out. By now the papers had picked up the story and everyone seemed to know that Love was having a contract dispute. He had a new agent who wanted his contract renegotiated. Pat talked with Bob and made him some promises. Things were going to be worked out. Pat told me everything was set, and Love joined us for the Hawaii trip.

When we got to Hawaii, Love told me that he had hurt his ankle and wasn't able to play. Following my policy, I sat him out. When we returned from the trip we had two more exhibition games on the west coast. I didn't play Love in those either. To me it was clear cut. When he told me he was ready to play, I would play him. He was my starting forward, a quality player. To the newspapers, it wasn't so clear cut. A couple of stories implied that I was not playing him because his contract disputes had not been ironed out yet. The implication was that I was sitting him out on orders from the front office. I ignored it. I knew why Love wasn't playing, and so did he.

Boerwinkle's knee had failed him again, despite his working it hard over the summer. We had to find a center before everyone in the league knew we were desperate. We didn't want to have to pay through the nose. In the first game of the season we hosted Philadelphia. They looked terrible. We looked almost as bad and it frightened me. We were lucky to hang on and beat them, and Philadelphia was a team that was to win just nine games all year.

When we played the Pistons at Detroit we were soundly beaten and we didn't look good. Finally it was time for a confrontation with Love. I hadn't worried a bit about his personal problems before because they had not affected the team and I figured he was working things out for himself.

When things don't go well on the floor and a player is obviously not playing his usual game, I ask him questions about his off-court life. "Bob," I said, "you're not playing good. We've been through too much together, we know each other too well. Are you sick?"

"No."

"Are you hurt?"

"No."

"Is everything ok at home?"

"Yes," he said. "My mind's not on the game. I've been lied to about my contract."

I was mad that he had let his personal problems affect the team. I told him he shouldn't have diluted his bargaining power by coming to training camp and committing himself. He agreed. I couldn't let him play until he was happy with his contract. I didn't know what the dispute was about, and I didn't care. At least not until the story broke in the paper the next day alleging that Love had been lied to.

Bob could feel the tension building on the team and he was afraid his negotiations might be hurting morale. "Maybe you should try to trade me," he said. I told him we'd try, but Pat couldn't get a fair exchange for him. We weren't about to give him away. There are few players in the league we'd take for Bob Love, and when nobody offered anyone substantial, Pat couldn't make the deal.

For the first time I got involved in a contract dispute. I told Pat that he should back out of the promises he had made since Love had virtually called him a liar in the press. I told him he should turn Love over to me. My plan was to assume that Love's contract was binding (which it was). If he wanted to play, he'd own up to it. If he didn't, I would suspend him. I didn't dislike the kid. I just knew he'd respond to the challenge and give up the fight so he could play ball.

Pat said he had to go through with Love's contract changes because he had given his word. I thought he could go back on his word since Love had blasted him publicly, but Pat would have no part of that. "Hell, if you renegotiate his contract you'll have every player on the team in here asking for a new deal," I said. "And they'll be damn fools if they don't." The contract was renegotiated.

I told Pat I wanted a raise. He laughed. "You know I can't do that, coach," he said.

"Pat, I've never been more serious in my life. I want a raise. If there's a bushel basket of money in the corner to be given away, I want my share. If you can renegotiate one contract, you can renegotiate another. I want a raise."

"Well, I can't give you a raise, but if you want more money you're free to look elsewhere."

"Let me get this straight," I said. "I am free to look for another job anywhere I want?"

"That's right. You have my permission." From that minute on I let it be known that I was looking. After all, Pat had signed my contract. He could give me permission to look for another job.

Clifford Ray became our starting center and we stayed with the same starting four otherwise. We looked frantically for a backup center and came up with Dennis Autrey of Philadelphia. As soon as he was on the roster, Tom had surgery and was lost for the season.

Around Christmastime Autrey was coming around

and I was about to give him more playing time to help spell Cliff. I didn't get a chance to work Denny in gradually, and I certainly had no option to change my mind once he was in. Cliff injured his knee and was out for much of the rest of the season and then a late injury put him out for the playoffs. Dennis was our center.

We won 51 games, but this was an all-different season than the one two years before when we had also won 51.

It hadn't been a building year, and it sure hadn't been a year free of problems as 1971-72 had been. The Bulls played hurt. They took up the slack for the loss of our two centers. To a man this team gave more than any other team I had ever coached. I pushed harder and demanded more of them and of myself than ever, and I think we all gave 100 per cent. We had finished second in our division for the third straight year, and again we would open the playoff season on the road. The problem was, we weren't sure where.

Milwaukee had won our division, and Los Angeles had won theirs, but their records had been identical. There was a big hassle over whether or not they would have a one-game playoff or flip a coin to decide who would play whom where. It was finally decided that they would flip, and the results sent us packing to play Los Angeles for the third year in a row. In a crazy decision by the front offices of the Lakers and the Bulls, we wound up getting about two hours' notice that we were to be on a plane to L.A. so we could play the Lakers the next night. I fought it, but the word was that we either play or forfeit. We were told Thursday that we were to play Friday. We didn't even have time to get the whole team assembled on the same plane. When we arrived, no practice court was available. We played and lost in overtime, and I guess I'll never know if our being rushed to L.A. had anything to do with the loss. I felt Pat had let us down by not insisting that the game be played a day or two later.

We lost the second game in Los Angeles too, and the press all but wrote us off. We were up to our old tricks again, losing every road playoff game and falling behind two games to none. They figured that since we lost in four straight the year before after 57 season wins, the Lakers would probably be able to wrap things up in short order with a couple more wins in Chicago. But we hadn't given up. I didn't know it yet, but this series would go to seven games. And as wild and bizarre as the last game would become, the focal point would really be the sixth game.

We surprised everyone in the basketball world by tying the series in Chicago. The playoff was becoming a replica of the 1970-71 series. When we got back to Los Angeles for game five, many of the Chicago reporters admitted in television interviews that they were surprised to be back in California. We weren't surprised.

The Lakers won the fifth game, keeping our string of road losses alive. Now the experts were sure the playoff was over. Chicago writers predicted that the sixth game in Chicago would be the last game. Elgin Baylor, the former Laker great, told the television audience that he figured the Lakers would end it in Chicago.

Maybe the experts had the thing all figured out, but I had an inkling that the Chicago fans might be holding on to the dream. Chicago people are unbelievable. They can make more noise than a full house

anywhere else in the league. I think it's because they
were raised baseball fans and they had to yell out-
doors for the Cubs and Sox.

Our type of team appeals to the Chicagoan. We're
aggressive. We stick up for our rights. We get technicals. The robust, loud, knowledgeable fan loves us.
He gets his money's worth. We play a simple, straightforward, Middle-America brand of basketball. We're
not cool, not sophisticated. We're Chicago. Hustling,
bustling, giving it all we've got.

Our games are mass therapy for the fans of Chicago. When I go out and hassle an official there are
hundreds of people in the stands who envision themselves telling off their bosses. And there are just as
many bosses in the stands who'll get on me for
hassling with an authority. They get their enjoyment
by screaming at me to "Sit down and shut up, ya
bum!" Kids love us because we hustle. Oldsters love
us because we play old-fashioned ball. When the fans
get behind us, we love *them*. That's what made the
sixth game of the 1972-73 playoffs one of the greatest games in my coaching career. Every game in a
playoff is a must. But this was the epitome. We had to
win just for the right to go back to the horrible Forum
where I couldn't remember the last time we had won.
The players were up. They felt they could win because they owed it to the fans and to themselves.

I felt the excitement building from the time I got
up in the morning. This was going to be a big, big
game in Bulls' history. I just knew it. When I got to
the stadium for my pre-game radio show the stadium
was almost filled already. As I walked to the press
table (inconspicuously, I thought) I was applauded.
That had never happened.

A little while later a couple of the substitutes came out to warm up. They were cheered. Chills ran down my spine. The house was filling up, the crowd was becoming restless. In the dressing room for a final chat before the game the electricity of the standing-room-only crowd could be felt all the way downstairs. It seemed as if the crowd and the court were right outside the door and we were somehow being kept from it in agonizing isolation. This was the essence of basketball. This was what it was all about. We and the Lakers were going to play the game the way it was meant to be played, before a full house in a do-or-die situation.

When we took the floor the cheering started. The noise hardly diminished for four quarters. Neither team led by more than four points at any time and every basket, every foul, every steal, every substitution, every timeout was met with thunderous gasps and cheers. It might as well have been the championship. I just loved it. I didn't want it to end. I wanted the lead to seesaw until we were tied at the end of every period. The thrill of winning that game was only tempered by the nagging disappointment that the game was over. Even if we had lost, I'd have been proud to have been involved. Chicago had backed us. We had come through. We had won the right to play the Lakers at the Forum in Los Angeles for the championship of the first round.

We were suddenly like an NCAA-bound college team. The whole season had come down to one game. This was it. One shot. The pressure's on. It couldn't be as intense as the sixth game had been (I had colleague's call and write to tell me it was the most intense game they'd ever seen) because it wouldn't be in Chicago. It would be in the Forum where the fans had come to expect the Lakers getting past the first round.

There wasn't a doubt in any of our minds that we would beat the Lakers. It simply had to be. We were ready. And we were high. The plane ride to California was exciting, filled with anticipation. In the game that old intensity came back. We were aware that thousands of Chicagoans were watching on television. We played it as if there would never be another game.

We were behind at the end of the first period but we took a slim lead into the locker room at the half. The third quarter, we felt, would be the key. It we could increase the lead, take the Lakers into the last period trailing, we'd have a real shot at them. The pressure would be on them. It worked. Moving into the last quarter the Lakers' work was cut out for them. They had to overhaul us, play great ball, force mistakes.

By now I was numb. We had played the same team seven straight games. There were no tricks, no secret weapons. We knew each other's strengths and weaknesses as well as we knew our names. We had to put our best against their best and hope that they'd buckle under the pressure. I would never blame a loss totally on the officiating, but I never could figure how the same Chicago Bulls team which played hard and aggressively in the first half and took 14 free throws, could play the second half even more desperately and not once get to the foul line. It was incredible.

But we still had a lead. Moving into the final moments it was obvious that Los Angeles was responding to the pressure. We weren't loose. We should have been but we wanted so badly to hang onto the lead.

We didn't want to blow it. The Lakers kept pouring it on. With 58 seconds to go they had pulled to within three points, but we had the ball.

Norm Van Lier had played a superhuman game and had scored 28 points. He brought the ball down and called our number one play. Norm could either shoot or pass to one of two players. We needed the bucket to put distance between us and the Lakers. If we scored we could use the 24-second-shot clock to our advantage.

Norm took the shot. Wilt Chamberlain lunged out from his position at the high post and got a finger on the ball as it left Norm's hand. The ball went straight up in the air. Jim MacMillan, a Laker forward, sprinted down the court as the ball dropped softly into Wilt's hands. The big guy reared back and fired a lead pass to MacMillan who laid it in. Our lead had been cut to just one.

We brought the ball up and ran a diagonal. The pass goes to Chet Walker who passes it to Bob Love when a screen has been set. Laker Bill Bridges fought through the screen and went over the top of Love to steal the ball. It was a foul. I can see that play in my mind as clearly as if it happened yesterday, and I still say it was a foul. With Love on the line shooting a pair I'm sure we would have been able to put the game away.

But the foul wasn't called. And while Bridges lunged for the ball, Gail Goodrich took off for the other end of the court. The lead pass from Bridges sailed over Goodrich's head. There was no way he could make a catch and get the breakaway layup. But he did. He caught the ball over his shoulder and flung it toward the bucket as he tumbled out of bounds. It had just the right twist and dropped through. The Lakers led by one and we had the ball with 26 seconds to play. Even if we scored at the end of the 24-second limit, L.A. would have the ball with two seconds to play. We brought the ball across the 10-second line and called timeout with 19 seconds to play, 17 on the shot clock.

We were numb. There was little to say. "We have plenty of time. Work the ball into Chet. We've got 17 seconds. Give us enough time to get a rebound, but not enough for them to score again. If we score they'll call a timeout and we'll talk about the defense then." I had nothing more to say. There were several more seconds left in the timeout. I crouched before the ballplayers who stared at me, anxious for any other little tidbit that would help ease the tension, make the shot go in, keep the Lakers from scoring again. The Forum was quiet. I was quiet. It was eerie. The whole season, the playoffs had come to this. Seventeen seconds and a prayer to make the winning shot. The mystery was unbearable. And the silence was weird. The horn blew, the fans cheered, we took the floor.

The pass goes in to Chet Walker. He kicks off to Weiss who is double teamed on the baseline in the corner. Weiss passes back out to Sloan. The seconds tick away. We're all standing. The crowd is screaming. Phil and I are shouting. The shot clock flash, flash, flashes as time runs out. "Five!" I scream. "Four!"

"Shoot the ball!" Phil shouts. "Shoot!" Sloan passes to Love and as the ball reaches his hands the buzzer sounds. It was absolutely unbelievable. It would have been a bitter loss to have missed the shot. But to not have even taken a shot. . . .

We were stunned. We walked to the dressing room silently as the Lakers accepted the roar of the crowd. The Bulls sat in their cubicles, heads hanging, breathing heavily. Not moving. I sat in their midst. There was nothing to say. We knew we had to chew this one before we could swallow it. We sat chewing and the taste was bad.

"That's a hell of a way to lose a season," I said finally. "It's not like us." It was strange, but we had no goat. Either we were all to blame or no one was. In the play where we could have scored, everyone had handled the ball. We shared the humiliation.

Still no one moved. I sat with my hands on my head. I began to realize that we had nothing to be ashamed of. We had gotten farther than anyone had expected. No one predicted that we'd even last five games against the defending champions. And how many teams could win 51 games after losing their starting center?

"We have nothing to be ashamed of," I said. "You've had a beautiful season. Don't let this last minute ruin your summer." Just five minutes after the end of the season, I started telling the players what each had to do to prepare for the next year. Then I went around to shake each player's hand as I do at the end of every season. By the time I got to Chet and Bob, they were already in the shower. I walked in with my shoes and street clothes on and shook hands with both of them. "Hey, Coach," Chet said. "We've had a hell of a good year."

I visited the Lakers' dressing room. Of course, the

atmosphere was a total contrast, but what hit me hardest was a message on the chalkboard. "Practice at 2:30 tomorrow." There would be no practice for the Bulls tomorrow. Wilt Chamberlain and Jerry West grasped what I was going through. Wilt told me he'd been there enough times to know. Jerry didn't say anything. He just gripped my hand and shook his head.

The team was to fly home the next morning, but I wanted to go home right then. I flew all night. I got home at about 7:30 in the morning, and told Janice, "Let's go someplace." At 10:30 we left for Disneyworld. I drove all the way to Florida, daydreaming about the last minute of that game. I gripped the steering wheel so tightly that my wedding ring cut into my hand. I was flat. After the demanding end of the regular season and the playoffs, suddenly we were through. There was no more.

CHAPTER **10**

CONFUSION

THE PHILADELPHIA 76ers, after winning just nine games, also won the coin toss for first choice in the college draft. Doug Collins, a guard we thought had the potential to be another Jerry West, was the logical top choice, and we wanted him. Pat Williams worked out a deal with Philadelphia, offering them Cliff Ray and Bob Weiss for the first pick. Philly agreed, the deal contingent on the condition of Cliff's knee. We went ahead and signed Collins, keeping the other involved names a secret until Ray had been examined. The 76ers insisted that their doctor see Cliff, and Pat agreed, on the condition that he come to Chicago without letting Cliff know what was happening. The last thing we needed, in the event that the trade didn't come off, was for our players to know they'd been on the block.

The Philadelphia doctor couldn't make it to Chicago, and draft day approached. Pat decided to fly Cliff to Philly for the examination. I thought that was crazy, and I told Pat so. I wanted Collins and I was willing to trade Cliff and Bob for him, but I couldn't have them treated like merchandise. "You can't just load that kid in a box car and send him off to the vet like a head of cattle. Wars have been fought over people being treated that way."

"I have to send him," Pat said. "I've given my word."

"Shit. Tell them the deal is either on the way it was, or the whole thing is off."

"I can't do that. We can't afford to lose Collins."

"Something stinks, Pat. If you send Ray to Philadelphia, you'll lose Collins anyway. At least send our doctor with him."

"Can't. Cliff's already on his way. It'll be all right."

Something was fishy. I knew somehow that everything was going to fall through, and now I was worried about the feelings of my ballplayers. By now they knew they were being traded, so if it didn't come off I was going to have two offended players on my hands.

Tuesday morning we learned that Philadelphia coach Kevin Loughery had quit at midnight. I was cold inside. I called Pat. "Cliff's in Philadelphia being examined right now," he said. "Call me back in an hour."

When I called back, Phil Johnson answered. "Pat's busy," he said. "And he's pretty sick."

"Cliff failed the examination, of course," I guessed.

"Yeah. He failed it."

I had taken Pat up on his earlier offer to look else-where for a job. I had talked with three other clubs and was anxious to leave, but when the Chicago owners heard about it they refused to let me break my contract. They insisted that Pat had no authority to let me look elsewhere. Pat and the owners had basic differences in philosophy and practice and hadn't been comfortable with each other since the sale of the club. He was a promotional man, but the owners were interested in the bottom line, the dollars and cents.

The front office was realigned and Pat was stripped of many of his decision-making responsibilities. I was given the responsibility of dealing with player per-sonnel including drafts, negotiating, signing, and salaries. Pat was to handle sales and merchandising.

Many of the Chicago sportswriters figured that I had undermined Pat because of some of our disagree-ments. It is not true. Oh, I could have slowed the changes a bit by refusing my new duties. No, I didn't go to bat for Pat. He admits that he wouldn't have survived under the new structure anyway. Within a matter of days he had his choice of offers and left to be general manager of the Atlanta Hawks. I sure got caught in the crossfire. Most people still believe that I somehow got him demoted and forced him out.

The writers also predicted that I would fail in my new job. They said one man can't handle both tasks, coaching and player negotiations. I didn't let that bother me. I've never had a job in my life in which failure hasn't been predicted for me. Why should someone else handle contract talks? I know my team better than anyone in the world. If there's someone who knows it better, he should be hired as the coach. I know who's valuable to me and in exact order how important each man is to the success of the Bulls. I dealt with the players and agents with that information in mind, and we cleared up most of the talks amiably and quickly. I think everyone was happy, except perhaps Bob Love's agent.

Love came back with yet another agent and wanted his contract renegotiated *again*. Three times in three years? The owners said no, and I agreed. Their policy was that they would not renegotiate contracts. If you open one, you've gotta open 'em all.

Love's agent put a lot of pressure on me in the press, but I wouldn't budge. I couldn't. Bob played it to the hilt and missed all of training camp and pre-season. I wasn't surprised. I fined him $50 a day and told him that if he missed any of the regular season the fine would continue and he would be suspended without pay. He reported in time for the last pre-season game and wound up having a great year. We had a hell of a party on his fine money. He was the guest of honor.

I've told my team many times, "I hope you never feel that you're worth the money you're getting. You're very fortunate to be in a situation where there is conflict between two leagues. More power to you. Get all you can. But don't let it affect your relationship to me or to this team."

These guys play hard and they can get rich if their agents don't steal their money. Many of the agents are little more than flesh peddlers who saw the salary war in pro basketball as a way to get rich quick. Salaries are skyrocketing to a point where several teams average over $100,000 per man in salary. Sometime I feel like I'm sitting on a keg of financial dynamite that will just blow wide open. Only three teams in the NBA make money. All the rest lose yet salaries keep climbing.

The agents clean up. Say a kid gets a three-year, no-cut contract for $120,000 a year. If the agent is taking just 10 percent (many take 15) he'll make $12,000 a year for three years on just one player. The player should be able to expect a lot of services for a fee like that. What do the agents do after the contract is signed?

If an agent is as concerned about the player's welfare as he says he is, he should take advantage of the credit power a man has who makes the kind of money NBA players make. He should advise the player to make investments which will set him up for the rest of his life. I'll be able to judge how good an agent is by where his clients are in 10 years.

I think I get along pretty well with the agents I deal with. We don't dicker much. They tell me what they want, and I tell them about what we can give. We don't give any money away.

When we thought we were losing Cliff to Philadelphia, we drafted Kevin Kunnert, a 7-2 center Phil and I had met at a developmental camp out west a couple of years before. When he and his agent met with Phil and me to negotiate, Kunnert came into the office in jeans and sandals. He slouched down on the couch and propped his feet on the corner of a chair. His agent began our "discussion."

"This kid is going to help you win the NBA championship this year," he said. It was what I expected to hear from an agent, but when I heard the phrase again and again in his monologue I started a slow burn. Kunnert didn't move. He was comfortable.

"Two things bother me," I said, interrupting. "First,

you must not have much respect for the NBA to think that your man can come in here and help us win the championship. The kid hasn't played a minute against a pro. Who knows how long it'll take him to become an effective player?

"Second," I said, turning to Kunnert, "if you're so great, why didn't your team win its conference championship?" His answer led me to believe that he was probably more of an individualist than a team player.

We discussed money and suddenly Kunnert said, "I'm worth 1.1 million."

I stared at him. I could hardly believe that I had heard him correctly. I probably would have been willing to go about $100,000 a year for two or three years. We had picked 12th. Had the first 11 teams made drastic mistakes missing out on this million-dollar talent? And the way he had said "one-*point-one!*" Point-one in that context is *one hundred thousand dollars.*

I glanced at his long, long legs propped up on the chair. "You know, it doesn't really bother me that you walk into my office with sandals on," I said quietly. "And it doesn't bother me that your hair is down past your shoulders. But what really offends me is that you've got both damn feet up on my chair."

He bolted to an upright position. "I was only trying to relax."

"Don't try so hard to relax around me. If you're fortunate enough to be a member of the Bulls' organization, and if you can contribute half as much as you say you can, I don't want you relaxed around me. I won't be much in your life. I only want two hours a day. When I'm on the court with you for those two hours, I don't want you practicing to relax." We traded his rights to Buffalo. He's now with Houston. Even if he becomes a superstar, I'll not regret my decision. I hire attitudes not bodies. You touch a whip to a jackass and he balks. Touch it to a thoroughbred and he responds.

We had a good training camp, but there were no rookies who could break into our lineup. Boerwinkle's operation had been a success, but he was not as mobile as I had hoped. Cliff Ray was eager to gun for the starting center job. He earned it and kept it all year. I had no trouble with either Cliff or Bob Weiss, even after the Philadelphia situation.

We blew off to a fast start, winning 15 of our first 20 games and stringing a dozen victories in a row. Unfortunately, the Bucks were just as hot and their winning steaks kept them ahead of the pack from start to finish. Detroit was our biggest nemesis, hot-shooting Dave Bing and big Bob Lanier keeping them in the race until the last few games of the season.

In late November Bob Cousy quit as coach of the Kansas City-Omaha Kings. It was the break Phil Johnson had been waiting for. He had had some feelers for other clubs, but here was a chance to turn a club around. The Kings hired him. I didn't envy him the job of starting in mid-year, but he did well. Kansas City-Omaha played nearly .500 ball for him the rest of the season, and he didn't even have a chance to get to know his players first. I had no doubts that Phil would do a great job for the Kings, especially after he gets to run pre-season training camp with them once.

Midway through the season I had a run-in with officials that really blew the lid off. We had lost to the Sonics in Seattle on a disputed call. I was furious.

On the way through the long tunnel to the dressing rooms I was told that one of the refs had been in our room before the game asking for tickets. That's strictly forbidden in the NBA. I caught up with the refs and demanded to know which of them had been in our dressing room. They wouldn't answer. I pointed my finger at one and thumped his chest. "I want to know which of you guys was in our dressing room!" I knew immediately that I had made a mistake. I figured I'd be hearing from the commissioner about it, but as I got to our dressing room I quickly forgot about it. Bill Russell, the Seattle coach, had expressed an interest in John Hummer, one of our forwards. John wasn't fitting into our system, so I wanted to make the deal.

Russell wanted Hummer to join the Sonics that night. I agreed and checked the parking lot to be sure Hummer hadn't already gotten on the bus. He hadn't. As I turned around, he came out of the coliseum. "Hold up, John," I said, "I've traded you to Seattle." I can still see big Bill Russell waiting in the shadows. The Sonics call the Hummer trade the *parking lot deal*.

A few days before the all-star break in Seattle I got a call at home from the commissioner. "When you gettin' to Seattle?" he asked. I misunderstood him. I thought he had asked "What'd you get in Seattle?"

"Oh, you wouldn't believe the shit I got in Seattle!" I said.

"I just want to know when you're getting to Seattle. I want to talk to you." Here I had already admitted my guilt!

He hit me with a $2,000 fine, the biggest ever, and also suspended me for a week, another first. I missed three games and Bob Biel took over for me. (We won

two of the three and I began to wonder how dispens-
able an NBA coach might be.)

We held our own the rest of the way, winning 54
games for our second best season and edging Detroit
out of second place.They had the fourth best winning
percentage in the league so we had the home court
advantage in the playoffs. They had played us close
and tough during the season, so we were going to
have to do well to get any farther in the playoffs than
we ever had. Here was our chance to get past the first
round for the first time.

We lost the first game and our home court advantage. Detroit was up, and we were in trouble. I knew
if we started hitting, we could beat them, but we had
never won a road playoff game. We couldn't let them
get a two-game lead on us.

We won the second game in Detroit in a battle
where the lead changed hands 21 times. It was really
something to see the Bulls win the games they had to
win. They had done it all year and I grew to respect
them more and more. After that it was a matter of
beating the Pistons at home three times while they
beat us on the road twice. The series was tied three
different times, but we made history beating the
Pistons by two in the final and advancing to the
playoff semifinals. Meanwhile Milwaukee had beaten
Los Angeles in five games and had lost only twice in
three weeks.

They blew us out of the first game in Milwaukee
and Abdul-Jabbar was the whole story. It became obvious that we were in for a rugged series, especially
without Jerry Sloan who had been injured in the sixth
game against Detroit.

The Bucks were playing super ball. If we were

going to win, each player was going to have to play above his season's average. We lost the second game at home by two, but the game wasn't really that close. Milwaukee had built a lead that our late rally couldn't overtake. We were down 2-0 in the series, and I would have bet anything that we would come back and beat the Bucks in Milwaukee in game three. They were so intimidating that we couldn't afford to lose. I wanted to motivate the Bulls. I took a chance, a calculated risk. "Some of you have already given up," I said. I was trying to reach a certain few, but two of the guys who really *had* worked their tails off were the ones who took offense. In trying to motivate some, I had alienated others.

We lost the next two and Milwaukee had shut us out. We had little to be ashamed of. The Bucks were even better than the record-setting Lakers (70-12) who had whipped us in four straight two years before. Milwaukee didn't have the great regular season record the Lakers had in 1971-72, but the Bucks beat us more handily.

A lot of coaches would give anything for four straight 50-plus win seasons, but we were at an impasse. Winning consistently is great, sure. And it's no disgrace to finish second four years in a row when you're finishing second to a team like Milwaukee. But what do you do as a coach? Do you settle for the 50 wins, a playoff spot, and second place? Or do you regroup, make changes, and try to get over the hump?

EPILOGUE

IF ANYTHING, the press image of Dick Motta worsened by the end of the 1973-74 basketball season. He had been ejected from several games, hit with numerous technical fouls, nailed with the biggest fine in the history of the league, and suspended. And he half expected to hear from the commissioner on an incident in the playoffs at Milwaukee in which he tossed his sport coat to the ref with a "you've taken everything else, you may as well take this too."

Following his year in the papers would have given you the idea that Motta was a mouthy, hard-driving, perhaps intelligent but humorless smart aleck. It would have been difficult to imagine him driving an old Karman Ghia, lounging at home in jeans and barefeet, or laughing with his wife and kids. The reporters wanted Motta to be a self-righteous, unbending man who defended his mistakes, took credit for victories, and hurled veiled barbs at his own players after losses.

When his aggressive "Monsters of the Midway" had a couple of rough and tumble games against the Milwaukee Bucks, writers and fans were reminded of the fearless defense the Bulls are known for. Speculation spewed forth about alleged pre-game meetings where Sloan and Van Lier were instructed to hack and grab and punch, and where Cliff Ray was told to foul anybody driving toward the basket "because we've got plenty of centers." When the team played poorly and a player said something about Motta in the heat of the moment, the dissension was reported. Writers asked Motta, "Don't your players like you?"

"This is no popularity contest," he'd answer, hoping against hope that the writer would know what he was trying to say. He came off like a guy who didn't care what his players, or anyone else for that matter, thought about him. It wasn't true, but he didn't have time to change the image. He heard the ridiculous questions and reactions to his answers and decided to disregard the press. "They don't know basketball," he'd reason. "What do I care what they write?"

But he did care. It was hurting his team. He had never talked about the press to the Bulls. But before a late season game against Philadelphia he felt he had to. "I know the writers have been hard on you," he said. "But I'm proud of you. I'll be able to look at myself in the mirror in 10 years and tell myself that this wasn't a dirty team, and that we never discussed how to get away with anything. Don't change your game, but remember that the officials read the papers too."

Motta expects his players to be responsible adults. He figures that since they accept their high salaries in good faith, he can expect a full performance in good faith. Basketball players are the highest paid professional athletes in the world. Some individuals from other sports will make more money, but the average salary of an NBA player is nearly twice that of any other pro sport. Even Motta, who is probably the third highest paid coach in the league, knows that three-fourths of his ballplayers make more money than he does. It could hurt him by costing him another wedge in discipline and control, but he has never expected to have authority handed to him on a silver platter.

Motta grabs authority by the horns and hangs on. He's never had a team at any level that hasn't tested him. "You can lose control of a junior high team as easily as you can a pro team," he says. "Anytime you deal with people, they're going to put it to you. The strongest will survive and the weak will float down the river. The minute these players feel that they are more important than the team, they've lost their usefulness to us. We have enough trouble during a season without having to worry about egos. It takes a humble guy to bust his tail for 82 games, regardless how much money he makes. The teams that are trouble-free are the ones that will win."

The human body and mind are not designed for 82 games of professional basketball in less than 6 months. With the air travel, the time changes, pace, and the abuse of the game, pro teams are not expected to play more than 50 good games in a season. Motta insists that over the last five years there haven't been more than a half dozen games each season in which he wasn't satisfied with the way the Bulls hustled. He feels his players are physical geniuses. "Somewhere around the age of ten or so," he says, "these men decided that they wanted to be excellent basketball players. Whether their reason was to get out of the ghetto, to fight hunger, to build their ego, to get away from their parents, or whatever, they have become single-purposed. They are narrow in their scope. They are the greatest. I compare them to musicians and artists. They are eccentrics who make big money. I don't take lightly the task of trying to get them to blend their talents into a working unit."

There *is* a light side to coaching, however. When Tom Boerwinkle was injured during the 1972-73 season, Motta let him travel with the Bulls on a few road trips to keep him from being completely frustrated. Tom grew a little beard, and with his seven-foot, 275-pound frame he was often mistaken as the leader of the Bulls.

That was fine with Dick Motta. He often enjoys staying several steps behind his team when walking through airports and hotel lobbies, just to see the re-action of people on the street. During one of those 1972-73 road trips, a stewardess asked Tom, "Are you in charge of this group?"

"Yes, I am," he said, in his most authoritative tone.

"Well, do you want any of the fellows to have hard liquor?"

"Oh, by all means no."

"It's time to eat," she said. "Should we wake up some of them?"

"Yes," Tom said slowly. "But, just wake up the ones that are sleeping."

She nodded thoughtfully and backed away.

At Chicago's O'Hare airport Motta kept his distance from the giants as they hurried through the terminal. As the Bulls waited for their plane, Motta stood with strangers. "Wonder who they are?" a man asked him.

"I don't know," Motta lied. "Maybe we ought to get their autographs."

The coach approached Boerwinkle. "Do you play basketball?" he asked. Tom broke up.

Often people recognize Motta, but because of his size they don't immediately think of him as coach of the Bulls. "Are you who I think you are?" someone will ask.

"Andy Williams?" Motta will say.

"No. No. Aren't you in sports?"

"Right. I'm the goalie for the Blackhawks."

Once a woman ran up to Motta in a restaurant and squealed, "I know you. I know you. You're famous aren't you?"

"Yes ma'am. I'm Harvey Gekouris."

"Oh," she said, her smile fading.

You'd think anyone would be proud to be known as an NBA coach. But Dick Motta will tell anyone who wants to know: he came to the Bulls through a series of lucky breaks, and any one of a thousand small-town coaches could have had the same success and may have even led the Bulls to a title by now. Some people believe that. Those who know basketball don't. Phil Johnson, who has been involved as a player or coach with every team Motta has ever coached, doesn't buy it.

Gene Visscher, who played for Motta at Weber State, laughs just thinking that anyone else could have done the same job in Chicago. "If there are a thousand coaches who could have done what Dick has, I'd like to know where they are," he says. "How come so few college coaches have been successful in the NBA?"

Then why would Motta say such a thing? False modesty? A feeling of insecurity? Perhaps both. Johnson, who feels he knows Motta better than any one else, says the coach is a fascinating dichotomy. "I think there's an element of insecurity in Dick," Phil says. "Maybe because he so enjoys his job and feels lucky to have it. But on the other hand, he has a great deal of confidence in his system and techniques."

Putting together a basketball team comprised of 12 all-American, spoon-fed, egotistical, high-paid giants is a very delicate and difficult job. It takes a man of contrasting moods to pull it off: a man who has supreme confidence in his system, believes in himself as a teacher, yet fears that he will wake up one day to find that he is a failure.

It's this contrast which is, I think, the genius of Dick Motta. He will be whatever he needs to be to impress you the way he thinks you need to be impressed. To a Chet Walker he is an admirer, an asker of questions, a seeker of advice. He envies Chet's championship ring. He thanks his lucky stars that a player of Chet's coolness and talent is so coachable. He won't yell at Walker. He doesn't have to.

To a rookie demanding too much money, a stubborn agent, a pesty reporter, Motta can appear cold, potentially explosive. Intimidating. His direct monotone tells them where they stand. There's a mystery about the man. Something about him makes them want to get to know him, or at least talk to him so they can pretend to know him. He's not close to many. People who have business with Motta are often surprised

that he is not a fiery-tongued serpent, quick to demand all the advantage, unbending.

What kind of a man is it who says he's coached in
better leagues than the NBA? A smart aleck? An
idiot? If he is quoted out of context, readers smile
and say, "There he goes again, saying something
ridiculous just to get attention."

But Motta believes it. When he says he's played in
better leagues he's not trying to make anyone believe
that the Big Sky Conference out West had even one
player who compares to the NBA superstars. Nor is
he trying to make anyone believe that the level of
competition approaches the team talent in the NBA.
But it *was* a more balanced league. The last place
team could blow you out. There were no Portlands or
Clevelands. Motta isn't writing off the NBA, but he
looks forward to the day when the expansion teams
are settled and competing on a par with everyone
else. "That would be real competitive basketball,"
he says.

It still awes him to be associated with the best basketball players in the world. Sometimes he has to
pinch himself to really believe that he's coached guys
like Chet Walker, Jerry Sloan, Norm Van Lier, and
Bob Love. He often talks of the thrill of having
coached against people like Jerry West, Oscar Robertson, Kareem Abdul-Jabbar, Wilt Chamberlain, and
Bill Russell. He doesn't take it in stride. The first time
he saw his name and picture in a Bulls' yearbook he
thought, *Even if I get fired before the season, no one
can take this away from me. I was in the NBA.*

Dick Motta would be happy to just be able to be in
the locker room with the Bulls and to see the anxiety,
the tension, and the emotion with which they prepare

for a ballgame. But to be able to teach them and coach them is a privilege he sometimes wonders if he's worthy of. He is awed by their talent and agility, and no matter how much he pushes, needles, cajoles, or goads them, they know he is on their side.

It hurts Motta when his players are not appreciated. He doesn't understand booing when his players are trying as hard as they can. In that way, he lives in a fantasy land. He's the perpetual daydreamer. He's working as hard as he can doing the very best he can, and then boos will shock him back to reality. He consoles himself and his team with, "They just don't understand."

When the Chicago fans lived up to the stereotype Motta had built for them in his mind, it was the highlight of his career in Chicago. For the first time in his coaching career his team was about to lose its fourth straight game. The Bucks were knocking them out of the playoffs. There would be no miracle finish, no patented Bull comeback this night. Milwaukee had laid them open and there was no time for healing. But the fans wanted to thank the Bulls for a year of exciting basketball. Trailing hopelessly with two minutes to go the Bulls were given a standing ovation by the Chicago crowd. Motta was visibly moved and will never forget it. He'd like to win a championship for people who appreciate you even when you lose. Those are his kind of people.

MOTTA'S RECORDS

Year	Team	League	W	L	Place in League
1953-54	Grace (Idaho) Junior High		9	1	First
1956-57	Grace (Idaho) High School		15	9	Second
1957-58	Grace (Idaho) High School		24	2	First
1958-59	Grace (Idaho) High School		24	2	First (also state champs)
1960-61	Weber Junior College	ICAC	11	1	First (8th in NJCAA)
1961-62	Weber Junior College	ICAC	11	1	First (12th in NJCAA)
1962-63	Weber State College	Ind.	24	2	
1963-64	Weber State College	Big Sky	17	8	Second
1964-65	Weber State College	Big Sky	22	3	First
1965-66	Weber State College	Big Sky	20	5	First
1966-67	Weber State College	Big Sky	18	7	Third
1967-68	Weber State College	Big Sky	21	6	First (to NCAA playoffs)
1968-69	Chicago Bulls	NBA	33	49	Fifth
1969-70	Chicago Bulls	NBA	39	43	Fourth
1970-71	Chicago Bulls	NBA	51	31	Second
1971-72	Chicago Bulls	NBA	57	25	Second
1972-73	Chicago Bulls	NBA	51	31	Second
1973-74	Chicago Bulls	NBA	54	28	Second